COFFEE POTS
and
TEAPOTS
FOR THE COLLECTOR

HENRY SANDON

COFFEE POTS
and
TEAPOTS

FOR THE COLLECTOR

ARCO PUBLISHING COMPANY, INC.
New York

Also by Henry Sandon
The Illustrated Guide to Worcester Porcelain
British Pottery and Porcelain for Pleasure and Investment
Royal Worcester Porcelain

Published 1974 by Arco Publishing Company, Inc.
219 Park Avenue South, New York, N.Y. 10003

Copyright © 1973 by Henry Sandon

Library of Congress Catalog Card Number 73–80766

ISBN 0–668–03337–1

Printed in Great Britain

Contents

ACKNOWLEDGMENTS

My grateful thanks are due to all who have assisted me in the preparation of this book, those who have provided information and photographs or allowed their pieces to be photographed. As well as the acknowledgements for the individual photographs, thanks are especially due to D. W. Allen, Brazilian Coffee Institute, Bristol Art Gallery, Ceylon Tea Centre, Mrs. Elizabeth Collard, Christie Manson and Woods Ltd., Folger Coffee Company and Procter and Gamble, Anton Gabszewiez, Geoffrey Godden, Mrs. Harriet Carlton Goldweitz, Derek Halfpenny, Japan Information Centre, Mrs. F. Shand Kydd, J. Lyons and Co., Ltd., Mulberry Hall Ltd., Phillips Son and Neale Ltd., Sotheby and Co., Stoke-on-Trent City Museum, The Tea Council, Victoria and Albert Museum, Winifred Williams and Robert Williams.

Especial thanks are due to John Beckerley who took the splendid colour photograph on page 111 and the black and white photographs of the Worcester pieces and to Neal French, who not only produced the fine drawings of teapots and coffee pots on pages 65, 71 but was the first person to inspire in me the love of these wonderful shapes.

Tea and Coffee

'Thank God for tea! What would the world do
without tea?–how did it exist? I am glad
I was not born before tea.'

Sydney Smith, 'Lady Holland's Memoir'

'After the coffee things ain't so bad'

Henry Herbert Knibbs, 'That Inside Song'

Plate 1
Still life oil painting by Juan
Zurbaran, Spanish, seventeenth
century. The painting depicts
delicate Chinese porcelain, the
decoration enlivened with white
enamels, the teabowls partly filled
with thin, clear tea, ready to be
drunk without milk.
Cincinnati Art Museum

Plate 2
A famous oil painting showing a
family taking tea, attributed to
Richard Collins in about 1730, the
Chinese porcelain teabowls and
cake dish being K'ang Hsi, all the
other items silver. Notice the
different ways in which the bowls
are being held, it almost seems as
if the painter has set out to show
that it did not greatly matter how
you held the bowl–daintily with
little finger out, boldy in the whole
hand or anxiously with fingers
around the footring.
Victoria and Albert Museum

Two things that draw East and West together in
communion are the beverages tea and coffee. Of the two,
tea has the longer history, although its use in the West was
preceded by coffee.

Tea has a very ancient history, some estimates putting
its first discovery in China at more than 4,000 years ago,
but like many of the world's great discoveries, its origins
remain unknown. Charles Lamb could usually be relied
upon to give a plausible account of the discovery of any
item that pleased him, like his marvellous account of
swineherd Ho-Ti's discovery of roast pork (where an
accidental burning down of his house which contained a
pig produced the first roast pork and led him to continue
burning down houses, thinking that this was the only way
to produce the delicacy). But even Lamb is silent about the
invention of tea.

Can we believe that it was discovered accidentally in
2737 B.C. by the Emperor Shen Nung through leaves
falling into a cauldron of boiling water?

Although its first discovery is lost in the mists of
antiquity, there is no doubt that by the beginning of the
Christian era tea drinking was widespread throughout
China. Its first use was mainly medicinal but by the time
that the first great publication on the subject was written
in A.D. 780 – the *Ch'a Ching* by Lu Yu – tea had become
accepted by the Chinese as a pleasant and wholesome
drink. China at this period was in many ways greatly in
advance of the rest of the world, although contact with
other countries was discouraged.

Tea had been heard of in the West but its first written
evidence does not come until 1559, in the second volume
of Ramusio's *Navigationi e Viaggi*, published in Venice:
'They take of that herb, whether fresh or dry, and boil it
well in water. One or two cups of this decoction taken on
an empty stomach removes fever, headache, stomach ache,

pain in the side or in the joints and it should be taken as hot as you can bear it. He said besides that it was good for no end of other ailments which he could not remember, but gout was one of them.'

Among the earliest travellers allowed into China were Jesuit missionaries who were attracted to the drinking of tea because it was a wonderful alternative to strong liquor: 'The water must remain no longer upon the tea than while you chant the Miserere psalm in leisurely fashion,' they said.

Interest in the products and arts of China and Japan were growing in the West throughout the sixteenth century and the small quantities of porcelain, silks, brocades, spices and tea that trickled back to Europe merely whetted the appetite. Most of the trading was carried out by the Portuguese and Dutch.

In England, the growing interest in all things Oriental led Queen Elizabeth to send Sir Robert Dudley with three ships and a letter of friendship to the Emperor of China in 1596, but this small convoy disappeared, unheard of again. Nothing daunted, in 1600 the Honourable East India Company was inaugurated which was granted a monopoly of trade in the East Indies. Although it took this trading company many years to establish themselves they were eventually to have a most important part to play in the development of tea drinking in the West.

The earliest tea came into England by a circuitous route – by Chinese junk to Java or Sumatra, brought by Dutch merchants to Holland from whence it was re-exported to France, England and Russia. The first positive reference to tea in England is an announcement by Thomas Garvey in September 1658: 'That excellent and by all Physicians approved drink called by the Chinese Tcha, by other nations Tay alias Tea is sold at the Sultaness Head a cophee house in Sweetings Rents by the Royal Exchange London.'

In 1660 the same Thomas Garvey issued a broadsheet, which showed that tea drinking was put forward as a cure for all ills: 'The Drink is declared to be most wholesome, preserving in perfect health until extreme old age,' and the paean of praise goes on to give the various ills that would benefit from drinking tea, such as headaches, stones in the kidney, ague, dropsy and scurvy. He ended his epistle by saying ' . . . all Persons of Eminency and Quality, Gentle-

Plate **3**
Remains of a tile picture signboard that hung outside the Dish of Coffee Boy Coffee house in Brick Lane, City of London in the late seventeenth century. Notice the typical silver coffee pot of the day, the coffee being poured into a handleless bowl (probably Chinese) and the other essential items in a coffee house – beer tankard, wine bottle, newspaper and tobacco pipes.
Guildhall Museum, London

Plate **4**
Fine Chinese *famille noire* wine
ewer and cover from which many
teapot shapes developed. Height
6 in.
Christie Manson and Woods

men and others, who have occasion for Tea in Leaf may be
supplied. These are given notice that the said Thomas
Garvey hath Tea to sell from sixteen to fifty shillings the
pount.'

It will be better appreciated how great was the cost of
tea when it is explained that with the decline in the value
of money since those days, a pound of tea from Mr. Garvey
would have cost the equivalent of something like £10 for
the cheaper variety and £30 for the most expensive. At this
sort of price, tea could only be afforded by the very rich
and it was generally drunk in the coffee houses or the court.
As Alexander Pope in *The Rape of the Lock* noted with half-
concealed sarcasm in referring to Queen Anne in Hampton
Court:

'Close by those meads, for ever crowned with flowers,
Where Thames with pride surveys his rising towers,
There stands a structure of majestic frame,
Which from the neighbouring Hampton takes its name.
Here Britain's statemen oft the fall foredoom
Of foreign tyrants and of nymphs at home;
Here thou, great Anna! Whom three realms obey,
Dost sometimes counsel take and sometimes tea.'

This poem is especially interesting in showing that tea
was pronounced 'tay' in England and it was probably not
until the late eighteenth century that our modern pro-
nunciation, 'tee', was used.

Coincidental with the great expense of the raw material
was the small size of the bowls from which the tea was
drunk. These teabowls enabled Europeans to drink their
tea in the Chinese fashion, holding the bowl between
finger and thumb. At first the teabowls were imported
from China and, unlike the Chinese method of making tea,
infused in a pot of boiling water. The Europeans used
small red-brown teapots made at Yi-Hsing and sent from
China with the crates of tea.

These teapots inspired Dutch and English potters and by
the last few years of the seventeenth century small red
stoneware teapots were being made by the Elers Brothers
in Staffordshire. As noted in Rackham and Read's *English
Pottery*, in the diary of Lady Celia Fiennes in 1698: 'I went
to this Newcastle in Staffordshire to see the makeing of the
fine teapotts, cups and saucers of the fine red earth in
imitation and as curious as that which comes from China,
but was defeated in my design, they comeing to an end of

Plate **5**
Chinese *famille verte* 'bamboo'
shape teapot of the K'ang Hsi
period, developed from the wine
ewer. The 'greenfamily' (*famille
verte*) refers to prominent use of a
brilliant green enamel in the
decoration; many European
factories copied this and the later
famille rose (pink). Height 7 in.,
circa 1700.
Christie Manson and Woods

their clay they made use of for that sort of ware, and therefore was remov'd to some other place where they were not settled at their work so could not see it.'

The hard stonewares were much better tea vessels than those made of delft (tin glazed earthenware) which was not sufficiently heat-resistant. Most high quality tearwares continued to be imported from the Orient at considerable cost and it was not until the European discovery of hard paste porcelain at Meissen in Germany, around 1710, that the first break in the Chinese monopoly is seen. The secret of making porcelain spread around Europe and led to a gradual lowering of the cost. Cream coloured earthenwares from England in the late eighteenth century brought good quality tearwares within the reach of the middle class.

The cost of tea was also brought down and even artificial substitutes were introduced. But the benefit of cheap teas at seven shillings a pound was somewhat offset by a heavy Revenue charge of five shillings per pound, irrespective of quality, which had been imposed in 1680. This led to the great days of the tea smugglers.

More troubles arose with another tax imposed by the British government on good quality tea in North America. The best quality East India Company tea had an imposed tax which upset the Colonists and in 1773 led to the famous Boston Tea Party. As one contemporary English newspaper, the *Morning Chronicle and London Advertiser*, of 22nd January, 1774, noted: 'A number of resolute men (dressed like Mohawks or Indians) determined to do all in their power to save their country from the ruin which their enemies had plotted, in less than four hours emptied every chest on board the three ships commanded by the Captains Hall, Bruce and Coffin, amounting to 342 chests, into the sea.'

The good quality teas of the eighteenth century were of

two main types, black and green – Thea Bohea and Thea Viridis, and although Europeans regarded these as two distinct types, they actually came from the same plant. The black was the fermented and the green the unfermented leaf, both coming from a plant which was a species of the camellia. These two main teas were divided into groups, as follows:

BLACK TEAS

Bohea which produced a dark mahogany colour

Congou producing a pale amber colour, or when mixed with Bohea, giving a pleasing blend

Souchong producing a light amber colour

Pekoe the finest quality, jet black and producing a pale liquid; often used as a blend with other teas

GREEN TEAS

Singlo and Twankay a refreshing tea

Hyson named after a Mr. Hyson, an East Indian merchant; of a blue colour

Gunpowder a small leaf and the strongest of the green teas, allowing four or five waterings

The artificial teas could be made from a great number of leaves, such as sage, balsam, balm, ribwort, currant and ash, and some of these were added to genuine teas to increase their bulk.

By the late eighteenth century tea drinking had moved from the Coffee House to the home and the tea gardens. Although the most famous tea gardens were in London – for example Ranelagh and Vauxhall – they also flourished in many towns. They even spread to America, where in New York the gardens were named after their London prototypes. Typical provincial tea gardens were those in Worcester known as Bird's Gardens, on the other side of the river from the porcelain manufactory. The following advertisement made the gardens sound most attractive, causing a local wag to refer to it as 'a bread and butter manufactory'.

'Worcester, June 30, 1781
At William Bird's, at Henwick Hill,
will be
A Public TEA-DRINKING,
at four o'clock,
On Friday next, the 6th of July.
Admittance into the Gardens One Shilling each person.
Music will be in waiting, as usual.'

Plate **9**
Silver coffee pot by Robert Timbrell and Benjamin Bentley made in 1714, on a Queen Anne stand and spirit lamp of 1709 made by Isaac Liger. Total height $11\frac{1}{8}$ in. It is the earliest octagonal coffee pot with stand and burner in America.
Folger Coffee Company collection of antique English silver. Courtesy of the Procter and Gamble Co.

Throughout the nineteenth century tea, retained its popularity as a drink and in the Victorian period it was established as a meal, with the addition of small tea plates to the tea service. But the most momentous happening of the century was the ending of the East India Company monopoly in the trading with China in 1833 which led to the increase of tea growing in other parts of the East.

The first growing of tea outside China was in Assam in Northern India, where the plant was found to be indigenous by Major Robert Bruce in 1823 and the first consignment was auctioned in London in 1839. Production later spread to Darjeeling and other areas and nowadays India and parts of Pakistan produce over 800 million pounds of tea a year.

Later tea growing was introduced into Ceylon, Java, Sumatra and Africa. Ceylon had been one of the coffee growing areas but at the present day the island has an annual production of about 500 million pounds of tea.

Tea drinking has now become international and an astronomical total of over 300 thousand million cups a year are consumed.

Coffee does not have such a long and complicated history. Like tea, its origin is shrouded in mystery but it would appear to have been drunk in Arabia as early as A.D. 600.

The most delightful account of the discovery of coffee is of a fifteenth century goat herd named Kaldi, who told the monks of a nearby monastery that his goats seemed to be especially frolicsome after eating certain berries – what might be called 'full of beans'. One of the monks decided to try the berries himself and, after boiling them he found that the drink helped him to stay awake during the long religious ceremonies. So its use by monks was very like the first use of tea.

By the early 1500's Turkish merchants had taken coffee from Arabia to Constantinople, and it reached Europe about 1585 when Venetian traders brought it to Italy. The first coffee houses were opened in Venice in the seventeenth century and the drink had reached England in 1637. By the end of the century London had hundreds of coffee houses and the drink had spread to France. The rest of Europe quickly took to coffee and its popularity was so

Plate **10** *(above)*
Silver teapot by Edward Penman, Edinburgh in 1721; the shape of the body is remarkably like the Meissen porcelain pot decorated in gold and silver (see Plate 44), showing the common influences between ceramic and silver shapes. *Sotheby and Co.*

Plate **11** *(above right)*
Very bold shaped Chinese blue and white teapot, made for the European market, the mounts, although apparently silver, are not hallmarked, being under the required weight. Much of this early Chinese porcelain was mounted in Europe and often the covers were chained to prevent them from falling off. Height 4½ in., *circa* 1725. *Private Collection. Courtesy of Geoffrey Godden*

Plate **12**
Silver teapot by Benjamin Pyne, 1705.
Sotheby and Co.

Plate **13** (*far left*)
Superb Elers unglazed red
stoneware teapot in imitation of
Chinese Yi-Hsing ware, moulded
sides, decoration in white slip,
spout and handle with silver
mounts and chain; possibly the
finest English earthenware teapot.
Height $4\frac{1}{2}$ in., *circa* 1690–1700.
Harriet Carlton Goldweitz Collection

Plate **14** (*left*)
Staffordshire lead glazed
earthenware teapot, possibly the
work of Samuel Bell or Thomas
Astbury, applied stamped reliefs in
cream colour slip, body highly
glazed. Height $4\frac{3}{4}$ in., *circa* 1735.
Harriet Carlton Goldweitz Collection

Plate **15**
Very fine large English saltglaze
teapot, superbly coloured and
modelled with a military scene
which might represent a battle in
the war of the Austrian succession
(Dettingen or Fontenoy) or
possibly the Jacobite campaigns.
Height 8 in.
*Christie Manson and Woods (now at
Colonial Williamsburg)*

great that in 1756 in Sweden its use was forbidden by law. A position was reached very like the bootlegging of the prohibition period and the law was revoked.

German society caught the craze and the great composer Johann Sebastian Bach wrote a humorous work about it called *The Coffee Cantata*.

The growing of coffee spread from Arabia to India, where a few precious seeds were smuggled by Moslem pilgrims, and to Martinique by a French captain, named de Clieu. From the latter seedlings coffee growing in the Americas is said to have originated and now there is 'an awful lot of coffee in Brazil'. This opened up North America to the drink and in the early 1600's Captain John Smith is said to have introduced coffee into Virginia. At the Merchants' Coffee-house, opened in New York in 1738, the American revolution is believed to have been hatched.

Our present day coffee bars and tea shops are calm, quiet places compared with their predecessors.

Coffee is now grown right around the world, in a broad belt ranging between the Tropics of Cancer and Capricorn. There are three main species of coffee tree: the 'Arabica', which produces the best quality beans and grows at an altitude of 2,000 to 6,500 feet; 'Robusta', a rather coarse species and the 'Liberica' which grows wild and has little commercial significance. It grows, like 'Robusta', at altitudes under 2,000 feet.

The ripe berries are very like cherries and usually contain two oval green seeds, the beans. These are picked by hand and, after various processes, the beans are dried in the sun. Cleaning, roasting and blending follow before the coffee is ready for use. Nowadays there has been an enormous demand for 'instant' or powdered coffee, but whatever type is used the drink certainly still has the same stimulating effect that it had on Kaldi's goats.

Plate 16 *(left)*
Silver coffee pot made by Paul de Lamerie, London. Characteristic of the bold ornamentation of this great silversmith, the decoration incorporates coffee sprigs on the border of the cover and beneath the spout. Height 10½ in. 1738.
Folger Coffee Company collection. Courtesy of the Procter and Gamble Co.

Plate 17
A superb Whieldon so called 'Ling Lung' redware teapot, inspired by a Chinese Yi-Hsing original, the cinquefoil body pierced while the clay was still wet, showing the cream slip behind, branch handle and prunus moulded spout. One of the great 'classical' very early eighteenth century copies of the Chinese. The pot can also be found lead glazed. Height 5⅝ in.
Sotheby and Co.

Plate 18
Astbury, Staffordshire, teapot of a most unusual type with applied reliefs in cream of the Royal Coat of Arms and the supporters, cover with flowers and leaves, surmounted by a crouching lion. Early eighteenth century.
Shand Kydd Collection

Plate **19**
Fine Staffordshire saltglaze pots of the first half of the eighteenth century, showing the two main types of handles – crabstock and round. All the pots are of plain round shape except for the two bottom row, right, which are modelled with pecten shells.
J. and E. D. Vandekar

Plate **20**
A group of fine Staffordshire
saltglazed teapots and a coffee pot
of the first half of the
mid-eighteenth century, showing
the variety of knob shapes to be
found.
J. and E. D. Vandekar

Plate 21 (*left*)
Staffordshire white saltglazed stoneware teapot, ovoid body with applied moulded decoration of vines which curl round the pot connecting it to the handle in the form of a hand, crabstock handle and spout, twig knob, traces of gilding remaining on the ornament. Height 4 in., *circa* 1730.
Harriet Carlton Goldweitz Collection

Plate 23
Rare Staffordshire saltglazed teapot with crabstock handle, spout unusually moulded with a stylised mask, boldly painted in *famille rose* enamels with flowering peony and gnarled rockwork. Height $4\frac{3}{4}$ in.
Sotheby and Co.

Plate 22 (*below left*)
Staffordshire saltglazed stoneware teapot, globular body, decorated with a band of incised lozenge ornament between two bands of scraps of clay chippings, handle in form of dragon, cover with lion knob surrounded by clay chips. Height $4\frac{3}{4}$ in., *circa* 1740.
Harriet Carlton Goldweitz Collection

Plate 24
Saltglaze teapot, globular shape with crabstock handle and spout. Brilliant enamel decoration of a flute player in a black tricorn hat, puce jacket and yellow breeches flanked by trailing sprays of fuchsia and other flowers below a green trellis diaper border edged with gilded scrolls. Height $4\frac{1}{2}$ in.
Sotheby and Co.

Plate **25** *(above)*
Three Staffordshire saltglaze
teapots, painted with birds in
enamel colours. The pot, top left,
has a crabstock handle and spout.
Height 5in. Top right, blue-green
ground enclosing a pheasant, $4\frac{3}{4}$
in. Below, a particularly unusual
shape, handle, spout and knob in
blue-green, 4 in. Early eighteenth
century.
Shand Kydd Collection

Plate **26**
Rare saltglaze jug and cover in the
form of Bacchus on a barrel.
Eighteenth century.
Tilley and Co. (Antiques) Ltd.

Plate **27**
Two most interesting Staffordshire teapots, produced from the same mould, slightly different in resultant sizes because of varying shrinkages; one unglazed red stoneware, the other lead glazed earthenware. Heights 3¾ in., *circa* 1735–40.
Harriet Carlton Goldweitz Collection

Plate **28**
Rare Staffordshire white saltglaze stoneware 'House' teapot in form of Georgian house, cover a chimney with bird finial, spout a serpent, handle a dragon. Height 5¼ in., *circa* 1745.
Harriet Carlton Goldweitz Collection

Plate **29**
Staffordshire white saltglaze miniature camel teapot in form of kneeling camel and howdah containing profile of man in window, head and neck of camel forming spout, handle a scaly serpent; the pot has great verve and assurance. Height 4 in., *circa* 1745.
Harriet Carlton Goldweitz Collection

Tea Drinking Ceremony and Coffee Houses

'Tea is like the East he grows in
A great yellow Mandarin
With urbanity of manner
And unconsciousness of sin'

G. K. Chesterton, 'The Song of Right and Wrong'

'Coffee (which makes the Politician wise,
And see through all things with his half-shut eyes)'

Alexander Pope, 'The Rape of the Lock'

The two great beverages led to two of the great social customs of the world – one Eastern and one Western. I feel sure that it will help towards a greater understanding of the development of the drinks and the vessels used if brief descriptions of the customs are given.

The Tea Ceremony is as different from Western ways of drinking tea as chalk from cheese. Developed from the practice of drinking tea by Zen Buddhist priests, who used tea much as Western students use coffee to help them to overcome drowsiness during long hours of meditation, it is easy to see the religious influence in the eventual ceremony. The cosy cup of tea in an English garden and the tea ceremony are poles apart. The following description has been given by the Japanese Ministry of Foreign Affairs and it is helpful to know the various objects used in the ceremony, some of these being highly prized and of great antiquity, brought along to be appreciated for their beauty and age.

Chasaku spoon made of bamboo or ivory for use in transferring powdered tea from the caddy to the bowl
Chasen whisk made of plain bamboo, which is used to beat or knead the mixture of powdered tea and hot water
Chaire tea caddy, a small receptacle for powdered tea used in the tea room; one of the most important articles
Chakin tea cloth, a small oblong piece of plain white linen used to wipe the teabowl
Chawan teabowl, invariably ceramic
Fukusa a small piece of silk, doubled almost square; two different pieces are used by the host, one hanging from his sash and the other placed in the bosom of his kimono

Plate **30**
The Tea Ceremony; notice the simplicity and calm, the utensils are described in this chapter.
Japan Information Centre

Plate **31**
Staffordshire white saltglaze teapot
in form of a pecten shell, a
favourite subject, with brilliant
gilding, snake spout with nude
figure riding astride. Height 5½ in.,
circa 1745.
Harriet Carlton Goldweitz Collection

Furo a portable charcoal brazier which is used during
the warmer season in place of the stationary fire box.
Futu-oki a small piece of China, bamboo or metal, on
which is placed the ladle or the cover of the kettle as the
occasion may require
Hishaku a ladle made of bamboo or wood; a bamboo
ladle is used in the tea room for the kettle
Kaishi pieces of white paper on which guests place their
cakes at a Chanoyu party
Kakemono a painting or example of handwriting mounted
as a hanging scroll
Kama a kettle to boil water, usually made of iron,
sometimes of gold or silver
Kamashiki usually an antique article or a fresh pad of paper
on which the kettle is placed when lifted from the hearth
Kan a pair of rings used to lift the kettle
Koboshi receptacle for waste water used in the tea room
Mizusashi water jar, usually of china ware; any receptacle
for fresh water used in the tea room
Sensu a folding fan, each guest is expected to bring one to
a Chanoyu party

In a Chanoyu party the object is to purify one's soul by
becoming one with nature and also to embody the Japanese
people's intuitive striving for recognition of true beauty
in plainness and simplicity. These aesthetic ideals apply to
the room in which the ceremony takes place, the garden
attached to the room, the utensils used and the decor of
the setting, such as a hanging scroll or an *ikebana* (flower
arrangement).

There are many ways of performing the tea ceremony,
according to the customs of the host; but basically a
typical Chanoyu party will run as follows:

A special small house is used, having a tea room, a
service room, waiting room and a garden path leading to
the entrance of the tea house, which is usually located in a
specially created wooded section of the garden proper. The
host provides the *chawan*, *chasen*, *chaire* and *chasaku*, as a
rule valuable works of art.

Clothes of quiet colour are preferred; on strictly formal
occasions men wear a solid colour silk kimono with three
or five family crests on it, and white socks; women wear a
crested kimono and white socks also. The guests bring a
sensu and a pad of *kaishi*.

Plate **32**
Staffordshire saltglazed stoneware
teapot with crabstock handle,
decorated in Chinese manner in
polychrome enamels, cover with
pink and green scale. Height 4 in.,
circa 1755.
Harriet Carlton Goldweitz Collection

The regular ceremony consists of four parts; first a light meal is served, then there is a short recess; then the main part of the ceremony where *koicha*, or thick tea is served, which is followed by the service of *usucha*, or thin tea. The entire ceremony takes about four hours, although the usucha service alone can be performed, requiring only one hour.

The guests, five in number, assemble in the waiting room. The host appears and conducts them along the garden path, about twenty feet long, to the tea room. At a point on the way there is a stone basin filled with fresh water. Here they wash their hands and rinse their mouths. The entrance to the room is very small, so that the guests must crawl through, thereby humbling themselves.

On entering the room, which is provided with a stationary hearth or a portable firebrazier for the kettle, each guest kneels in front of the alcove and makes respectable obeisance. Then with his folding fan before him, he admires the hanging scroll on the wall of the alcove and the tiny incense holder on a side shelf. Next he looks in the same manner at the hearth or the brazier.

When all the guests have finished viewing these articles, they take their seats, the principal guest taking the one nearest the host. After the host and guests have exchanged greetings, the light meal is served, concluding with sweets.

At the host's suggestion, the guests retire to a waiting bench outside in the inner garden near the room.

A metal gong hung near the room is sounded by the host to signal the beginning of the main ceremony, the usual custom being to give five or seven strokes. The guests arise and listen attentively to the sound. After repeating the formality of purification at the basin, they again enter the room.

The bamboo screens hung outside the windows are removed by an assistant in order to brighten the surroundings. The hanging scroll is gone and in the alcove there is a vase of flowers. The *mizusashi* and *chaire* are in position before the host enters carrying the *chawan* containing the *chasen* and *chasaku*. The guests inspect and admire the flowers and the kettle and the host retires to the service room and soon returns with the *koboshi*, the *hishaku* and the *futu-oki*. He or his assistant carries out a cake container, placing it in front of the principal guest. The host then wipes the *chaire* and the *chasaku* with the *fukusa*

Plate **33** (*right*)
Rare white saltglaze teapot of almost octagonal pear shape, head of a serpent forming spout and its tail the handle, moulded on one side with a view of Portobello, captured in 1739 with Admiral Vernon's six ships, cover with lion knob. Height 5½ in., *circa* 1739–40.
Sotheby and Co.

Plate **34** (*far right*)
Wedgwood/Whieldon teapot of lobed vegetable form, the sides applied with leafing branches and with floret moulded spout and handle, the whole streaked in ochre, green and manganese on a cream ground. Silver mounted spout and chained cover. Height 6 in., *circa* 1745.
Phillips Son and Neale

Plate **35**
A group of three superb Staffordshire teapots of Whieldon type (similar examples can be seen in the colour plates). Top, six sided, moulded with Chinese women, covered with a brilliant green glaze. Height 5½ in. Below, left, a melon, glazed in natural colours. Right, formed of overlapping leaves, continuing into the cover, the knob in the form of a rabbit. *Circa* 1745.
Shand Kydd Collection (acknowledgement to Frank Tilley, FRSA)

and washes the *chasen* in a bowl of hot water drawn from the *kama* with the *hishaku*. He empties the bowl, throwing the water into the *koboshi* and wipes the bowl with the *chakin*.

The host lifts the *chaire* and the *chasaku* and puts *matcha* (three spoonfuls per guest) into the *chawan*. *Matcha* is made from the young leaves of tea plants twenty to seventy years old. He then takes a dipperful of hot water out of the kettle, putting about one-third of it into the *chawan* and returning the remainder to the *kama*. He then whips up the mixture with the *chasen* until it thickens, resembling a very thick green pea soup. The tea thus made is called *koicha*.

The host puts the *chawan* in its proper place by the hearth of the brazier and the principal guest, who has since eaten his cake moves along on his knees to pick up the *chawan*. The guest makes a bow to his fellow guests and puts the *chawan* on the palm of his left hand, supporting one side of it with his right hand. After taking one sip, he praises its taste, then takes two or more sips.

He wipes the part of the *chawan* from which he has drunk with the *kaishi* paper, and passes the *chawan* to the second guest and so on until all five have partaken of the tea. The last guest gives the *chawan* to the principal guest, who returns it to the host.

Usucha differs from *koicha* in that the *matcha* used in the former is made from the young tea leaves of plants only three to fifteen years old. This makes a foamy green mixture.

The rules used in the *usucha* ceremony are similar to those of the *koicha*, the main differences being: the *chawan* is a little smaller, the tea is made individually for each guest with two and a half spoonfuls of *matcha*. Each guest is expected to drink his entire portion; the guest cleans the part of the *chawan* which touched his lips with the fingers of his right hand and then wipes his fingers on the *kaishi* paper.

After the host has carried the utensils out of the room he makes a silent bow to the guests, denoting that the ceremony is over. The guests leave, seen off by the host.

The earliest known newspaper advertisement for coffee appeared in 1657, in the *London Public Advertiser* of 19th-26th May. Like the early advertisements for tea, it extolled the

medicinal advantages of coffee, in the following words:

'In Bartholomew Lane on the back side of the Old Exchange, the drink called Coffee (which is a very wholesome and Physical drink) having many excellent vertues, closes the Orifice of the Stomack, fortifies the heat within, helpeth Digestion, quickneth the Spirits, maketh the heart lightsome, is good against Eye-sores, Coughs, or Colds, Rhumes, Consumptions, Head-ach, Dropsie, Gout, Scurvie, King's Evil and many others is to be sold in the morning, and at three of the clock in the afternoon.'

The first coffee house to be opened in London is believed to have been that of Pasqua Rosee in 1652, as is noted in a broadsheet in the British Museum: 'Vertue of the COFFEE Drink First publiquely made and sold in England . . . in St. Michael's Alley in Cornhill by Pasqua Rosee at the Signe of his own Head.' From this time coffee houses increased in popularity until they reached their zenith in the eighteenth century. In 1739, within the area covered by Bills of Mortality (mainly the Cities of London and Westminster), there were 551 coffee houses, vying with 207 inns, 447 taverns, 5,975 beerhouses and 8,659 brandy-shops.

Plate **38**
Three typical earthenware Astbury/Whieldon type wares. Left, a solid agate tea caddy, 5½ in. Centre, a lead glazed redware teapot, applied stamped reliefs in cream colour slip, 3¾ in. Right, black lead-glazed coffee pot on typical feet, 9 in. *Circa* 1740–50. *Stoke-on-Trent City Museum*

Plate **39**
Staffordshire saltglaze coffee pot, decorated with 'Littler's' blue and floral gilding (blue slip painted over in opaque white enamels). Height 8 in., *circa* 1750. *Stoke-on-Trent City Museum*

Coffee houses, as the following quotations show, had a great number of uses:

Dispensing of coffee, tea and light refreshments

'Spencer's Breakfasting Houses – This is to give notice to all ladies and gentlemen, at Spencer's original break-fasting hut, between Sir Hugh Myddelton's Head and St. John-street-road, by the New River side, fronting Sadler's Wells, may be had every morning, except Sundays, fine tea, sugar, bread, butter and milk, at fourpence per head; coffee at three-half-pence per dish. And in the after-noon, tea, sugar and milk, at threepence per head, with good attendance. Coaches may come up to the farther garden door, next to the bridge in St. John-street-road, near the Sadler's Wells back gate.

'*Note* – Ladies, etc., are desired to take notice that there is another person set up in opposition to me, the next door, which is a brick house, and faces the little gate by the Sir Hugh Myddelton's, and therefore mistaken for me; but mine is the little boarded place by the river side, and my back door faces the same as usual: for

I am not dead, I am not gone,
Nor liquors do I sell;
But, as at first, I still go on,
Ladies, to use you well,
No passage to my hut I have,
The river runs before;
Therefore your care I humbly crave,
Pray, don't mistake my door.
Yours, to serve, S. Spencer.'
Daily Advertiser, 6th May 1745

Political meeting houses

'I first of all called in at St. James's, where I found the whole outward room in a buz of politics. The speculations were but very indifferent towards the door, but grew finer as you advanced to the upper end of the room and were so very much improved by a knot of theorists, who sat in the inner room, within the steams of the coffee-pot, that I heard the whole Spanish monarchy disposed of, and all the line of Bourbon provided for in less than a quarter of an hour.'
The Spectator, 12th June 1712

Plate **40**
Staffordshire saltglazed stoneware teapot, white body decorated in black with heraldic ermine design, reserve panels painted with 'Fred Prussiae Rex' and reverse with Prussian Eagle – Frederick, King of Prussia, was England's ally during the seven year war against France. Height 3¾ in., *circa* 1756–60.
Harriet Carlton Goldweitz Collection

Plate **41**
Staffordshire 'Drabware' saltglaze teapot, applied reliefs in white pipe clay and some ornaments of blue stained clay, twig finial in white clay. Height 4 in., *circa* 1740.
Harriet Carlton Goldweitz Collection

38

Reading newspapers and discussing news

'In London there are a great number of coffee houses most of which are not over clean or well furnished owing to the great number of people who resort to these places and because of the smoke which would quickly destroy good furniture. In these coffee houses you can partake of chocolate or tea or coffee, and all sorts of liquors, served hot, also in many places you can have wine or punch or ale. What attracts enormously are the gazettes and other public papers . . . workmen habitually begin the day by going to a coffee house in order to read the latest news.'
Cesar de Saussure, in 1725

Marriage bureau accommodation addresses

'A GENTLEMEN who hath filled two succeeding seats in Parliament, is near sixty years of age, lives in great splendour and hospitality, and from whom a considerable Estate must pass if he dies without issue, hath no objection to marry any Widow or Single Lady, provided the party be of genteel birth, polite manners, and five, six, seven, or eight Months gone in her Pregnancy. Letters directed to—Brechnock Esq., at Will's Coffee House, facing the Admiralty, will be honoured with due attention, secrecy, and every possible mark of respect.'
Public Advertiser, 16th April 1776

Accommodation addresses for lost and stolen goods

'LOST on Sunday last from a lady's side at St. James's Church a plain gold watch. Whoever brings it to Tom's Coffee House in Spring Garden Charing Cross shall have two guineas reward and no questions ask'd.'
Daily Courant, 21st February 1711

General advertisements

'Masquerade Habits to be Let, at Five Shillings per habit, the greatest Variety of any Place soever, being very Curious and Comick, at Tom's Coffee house, next door to Young Man's Coffee house Charing Cross.'
Daily Post, February 1725

The great London clubs

'Thence I went with Muddiman to the Coffee-House, and gave eighteen pence to be entered of the Club.'
Samuel Pepys's Diary, 8th January 1659–60

Plate **42**
Unglazed red stoneware teapot of octagonal form, moulded with an adaptation of a Chinese pattern known as 'Boy in a Tree', leaf topped snake handle, wrapped leaf spout. Height $3\frac{1}{4}$ in., *circa* 1754.
Harriet Carlton Goldweitz Collection

Plate **43** *(far right)*
Unglazed red stoneware teapot, globular shape with crabstock handle and spout, applied (sprigged) relief of formal foliage and a king and queen, possibly commemorating George III and Queen Charlotte's marriage in 1761, although an earlier punch pot has similar decoration depicting William and Mary (Rackham and Read *English Pottery*, Pl. 86, Fig. 154). Height 4 in., *circa* 1761.
Harriet Carlton Goldweitz Collection

Plate **44**
Rare Meissen teapot with wishbone handle and curious curved octagonal spout, silver decoration of flowers on a chocolate-brown ground. The spout and rim are decorated in gold; it is very rare to find both silver and gold decoration used on one piece. Height $6\frac{3}{4}$ in. Mark, crossed swords in underglaze blue.
Sotheby and Co.
(Compare the shape with the silver pot made by Edward Penman, Plate 10)

Plate **45** (*far left*)
Whieldon black lead glazed earthenware teapot on three mask and claw feet, spread winged bird finial, decorated with vine and grapes in applied relief and traces of gilding. Height 4½ in., *circa* 1750.
Harriet Carlton Goldweitz Collection

Plate **46** (*left*)
Staffordshire 'Ochre' lead glazed teapot of Astbury/Whieldon type, unusual pinched looped twig finial on cover, deep ochre coloured body, applied sprays touched with manganese-purple and green, handle, spout and finial in white clay. Height 4 in., *circa* 1740–50.
Harriet Carlton Goldweitz Collection

Plate **47** (*centre*)
Staffordshire 'solid agate' teapot, very beautiful pattern of veining over a light cream earthenware body, veined in vertical pattern with blue and rust brown. Height 3¾ in., *circa* 1750.
Harriet Carlton Goldweitz Collection

Plate **48** (*far left*)
Staffordshire 'solid agate' lead glazed teapot, on three mask and claw feet, coloured veining on cream ground by mixed clays, Chinese lion knob. Height 4¼ in., *circa* 1745.
Harriet Carlton Goldweitz Collection

Plate **49** (*left*)
Staffordshire lead glazed earthenware teapot, applied reliefs touched with green and manganese under the glaze – a good example of powdered oxides which have dripped down during the firing. Height 3¼ in., *circa* 1750.
Harriet Carlton Goldweitz Collection

Establishments for early fire, shipping and life insurance arrangements

'On Tuesday the 8th November next, Bennet's Coffee House in Plimouth, will be exposed to Sale by Inch of Candle, 3 Ships with all their Furniture; the names whereof are the Teresa, the St. Thomas, and the Palmo, two of 400 Tuns and the other 100. The Inventories thereof to be seen at Lloyd's Coffee House in Lombard Street, London. The said Ships are enter'd out for Barbados or Virginia.'
The London Gazette, 20th-24th October 1692
(Lloyd's Coffee House was to develop into the famous insurance and shipping firm of Lloyds of London.)

Early post offices

Coffee houses played an important part in early postal deliveries in London; as early as 1680 a Penny Post was established in Mr. Barker's Coffee House by William Dockwra, and in Mrs. Hannah's Coffee House by Robert Murray. Even after suppression of the Penny Post by the government in 1682, coffee houses were used as postal collections on holy days: 'Such persons who write Letters then are directed to leave them at those Coffee Houses known to be appointed by the Office, that they may be collected and delivered in due time.'
The London Gazette for 29th March to 2nd April 1683

The sale of coffee and provisions

'At the Coffee House in Exchange Alley is sold by Retail the right Coffee-powder, from four shillings to six shillings per pound, as in goodness; that pounded in a mortar at three shillings per pound; also that termed the right Turkie Berry, well garbled, at three shillings per pound – the ungarbled for less; that termed the East India Berry at twenty pence per pound, with directions gratis how to make and use the same. Likewise, there you may have Tobacco, Verinas and also Sherbets (made in Turkie) of Lemons, Roses and Violets perfumed; and Tea according to its goodness, from six shillings to sixty shillings per pound. For all of which, if any Gentleman shall write or send, they shall be sure of the best as they shall order; and to avoid deceit, warranted under the House Seal – viz. Morat the Great etc.'
Mercurius Publicus 12th-19th March 1662

Purveyors of quack medicines

'The Right, New, Cold-Drawn Linseed-Oyl, which is so famous for the'distempers, Phthisick, colds, and the only remedy for the Plurisie, is drawn by J. L., being the first author who put the same Oyl to be sold, at first at the Rainbow Coffee House in Fleet Street, but is now sold at Mr. Batson's and at Sam's Coffee-house by the Custom-House, and Say's on Ludgate Hill at Two shillings a pint bottle.'
Quacks of Old London – Thompson

Early gaming and card playing houses

'There are other little coffee houses much frequented in this neighbourhood – Young Man's for officers, Old Man's for stockjobbers, pay-masters and courtiers, and Little Man's for sharpers. I never was so confounded in my life as when I entered this last. I saw two or three tables full at faro, and was surrounded by a set of sharp faces that I was afraid would have devoured me with their eyes. I was glad to drop two or three half-crowns at faro to get off with a clear skin; and was overjoyed I so got rid of them.'
Journey through England, by Mackay

General and political meeting houses

'We rise by Nine, and those that frequent great Men's Levees find Entertainment at them till Eleven, or, as in Holland, go to Tea-Tables. About Twelve the Beau-Monde assembles in several Chocolate and Coffee Houses: The Best of which are the Cocoa-Tree and White's Chocolate Houses, St. James's, the Smyrna, Mrs. Rochford's and the British Coffee-Houses, and all these so near one another, that in less than an Hour you see the Company of them all . . . I must not forget to tell you, that the Parties have their different Places, where, however, a Stranger is always well receiv'd; but a Whig will no more go to the Cocoa-Tree or Ofinda's, than a Tory will be seen at the Coffee-House of St. James's.'
Journey through England, by Mackay

Coffee houses were put to all these and many other uses in London which continue to this day in the form of clubs, insurance and shipping houses. Now coffee houses are used for the actual drinking of coffee, although they are still meeting places, especially for younger people.

Plate **50**
Extremely rare and beautiful Meissen teapot of depressed globular shape, painted within shaped oval panels with Chinoiserie subjects, probably by J. G. Heroldt, within an elaborate baroque scrollwork border in semi-lustre, iron-red and gold. Cover, spout and handle painted with *indianische blumen*. Height 6 in. Rare K.P.M. and crossed swords mark in underglaze blue and gilded numeral.
Sotheby and Co.

Plate **51**
A beautiful Meissen teapot and tea caddy (sometimes called teapoys) finely painted in iron-red in the style of Kakiemon; crossed swords mark in underglaze blue and impressed repairers mark of Schiefer, who worked at Meissen in the first half of the eighteenth century. (Repairer was the name given to the craftsman who assembled complicated figure and other shapes.)
Sotheby and Co.

Plate **52**
Rare Du Paquier period Vienna teapot with unusual drum shaped cover, a mask of Pierrot in relief below the short, stumpy spout, handle joined to shoulder with a shell motif in imitation of silver cut-card work, enamelled with prunus, chrysanthemum and peony decoration. Height $4\frac{3}{4}$ in., *circa* 1720.
Sotheby and Co.

Plate **53**
Three fine European eighteenth century porcelain vessels. Left, Nymphenburg milk jug painted with an orangerie and formal Italianate garden. Height 6 in., impressed shield mark and D. Centre, Vienna pear-shaped coffee pot, cover with apple knob, finely painted *en grisaille* with ruins and village scenes. Height $9\frac{1}{2}$ in. Right, a Fürstenberg cylindrical chocolate pot finely painted with a bust portrait of a man in a circular medallion, wooden handle at the side as in most early coffee pots. Height 5 in. F & Z marks in blue, impressed numerals 2G.
Sotheby and Co.

Plate **54** *(left)*
Rare Capo di Monte coffee pot of baluster shape with crabstock handle, the body decorated in low relief with applied sprays of daisy-like flowers in gilding, cover with inverted teardrop knob. This type of pot more usually has Fukein type prunus blossom in relief. Height 10⅝ in. Mark, large *fleur-de-lys* in blue, mid-eighteenth century.
Sotheby and Co.

Plate **55** *(above right)*
Tournai coffee pot with bird's head spout, painted in a vivid tone of blue and gilding with birds after Buffon, the names of the birds inscribed on the base. Height 11½ in., probably second half of eighteenth century.
Sotheby and Co.

Plate **56** *(above, far right)*
Ansbach porcelain coffee pot of pear shape with elaborate scroll handle and mask spout picked out in colours, painted with birds in landscape with a farm in the background and surrounded with scattered insects and sprays of fruit, pear knob. Height 9 in. Mark A in underglaze blue, *circa* 1760.
Sotheby and Co.

Plate **57**
Beautiful Hague porcelain service. The factory at The Hague not only made their own soft paste porcelain but also decorated quite a lot of wares from other factories, notably Tournai. *Circa* 1770.
F. Th. Roeters Van Lennep

Tea and Coffee Pot shapes

'Like a small grey coffee pot sits the squirrel'

Humbert Wolfe 'The Grey Squirrel'

TEAPOTS

The Chinese first made tea in the teabowl but by the sixteenth century the drink was being infused in a teapot.

The first Chinese teapots to reach Europe were probably the red brown stoneware pots made at Yi-Hsing, near Soochow. It is thought that many were sent with the chests of tea possibly packed in sago, and there is no doubt that they greatly influenced Europeans. At first the shapes were copied in silver but towards the end of the seventeenth century the Dutch potters had begun to make teapots.

Holland at that time was the great home of tin glazed earthenware, called delft, as so much of it was made in the town of Delft. This material was used in an attempt to copy the greatly admired quality of whiteness in Chinese porcelain. Not yet able to manufacture porcelain, the Delft potters used a light coloured earthenware and covered it with an opaque tin glaze. This gave the appearance of being white porcelain but the ware was so soft that it was not really suitable to resist hot liquids. So although a very small amount of teaware was made in delft, an alternative had to be found and the answer was a hard red stoneware.

Stoneware clays are abundant in certain parts of the world and it was to North Staffordshire in England that the Elers brothers, Dutch emigrant potters, moved from Fulham in London. There they had made stoneware in the early 1690s, which brought a lawsuit down upon their ears in 1693 from Dwight, the Fulham stoneware potter, for infringement of his copyright.

In Staffordshire they discovered marvellous beds of clay suitable for making red stoneware, a body that could be made extremely thin, did not require glaze and yet was hard enough to resist hot liquids. This was to have a big effect on the history of English and world ceramics.

These early stoneware teapots were similar to the Yi-Hsing shapes and an example is shown in plate 13. This,

Plate 58
Staffordshire 'tortoise-shell' teapot, possibly Whieldon, applied relief under the glaze, crabstock handle and simple shell spout, cover with diaper and bamboo. Height 4 in., *circa* 1755.
Harriet Carlton Goldweitz Collection

Plate 59
Staffordshire 'tortoise-shell' teapot, three mask and paw feet, applied vines, leaf and grapes in style of early Whieldon school. Height 3¾ in., *circa* 1750.
Harriet Carlton Goldweitz Collection

Plate 60
Staffordshire 'tortoise-shell', lead glazed teapot, probably Whieldon, light brown mottled glaze, vine leaves and grapes in relief. Height 4 in., *circa* 1750.
Harriet Carlton Goldweitz Collection

almost certainly an Elers redware vessel, has a depressed globular shape with a high foot, a large loop handle and a small curved spout. The surface is moulded with sprays of flowering prunus, picked out in white enamel and with dots and insects between borders and dots, all painted in the same white enamel. The same type of decoration can be found on red stonewares attributed to Böttger at Meissen but was more probably by de Milde in Holland. Also it is found on a tankard dated 1706 and on a teapot in the Victoria and Albert Museum, and is thought to be the work of a Dutchman working in Staffordshire (see *Transactions of the English Ceramic Circle, vol. 2, no. 8.*).

This teapot shows two especially interesting features. The first is the exaggerated and strange proportions of Chinese type handles and spouts; this was to develop even more strongly in Chinese round bodied teapots, which almost invariably have a huge curving handle and a short, straight, pointing spout, so unlike the better balanced proportions of the typical European style, see the Worcester teapot, (plate 76). The second feature is the care with which presumably the original owner of the teapot has protected the spout from getting chipped by a silver mount and prevented the cover from falling off while in use by a silver chain.

Throughout the eighteenth century covers were a great problem; they were, of course, made separately from the pot and hardly ever fitted tightly after firing. It was not until the first years of the nineteenth century that designers managed to solve this problem with the provision of special locking slots.

Many other potters produced Chinese style teapots in succeeding years. The more important of these were the small round old stoneware pots produced by Böttger at Meissen, the redware so-called 'Ling Lung' pots by Whieldon, inspired by another Chinese Yi-Hsing shape having a cinquefoil body pierced with flowering branches and with a branch handle, this also being produced in lead glazed earthenware (*English Pottery by Rackham and Read, plate 89*) and, by the same Staffordshire potter, octagonal pots moulded all over with an adaptation of a pattern called 'Boy in a Tree'.

It is natural that when artists and craftsmen first start to make something they should tend to copy the original inventors. So, for some years, all teawares made in Europe

Plate **61**
Rare tea kettle and stand for a heater to go underneath, all in Dutch Delft, painted in blue. G V S mark of G. Verstelle, third quarter of eighteenth century. *Victoria and Albert Museum*

were based upon the Chinese. Soon most of Western
Europe was using teapots and drinking tea from the
teabowls that were either Chinese or possible European
copies.

Some shapes developed in Staffordshire which copied
the more extravagant Chinese forms of houses (plate 28),
camels (plate 29) and squirrels (plate 147) and the making of
strange teapot forms was continued into the early days of
English porcelain factories, as witness the globe artichoke
pots from Longton Hall (plate 68). Strange forms were to
emerge again in the high Victorian period (plate 149) and I
am often asked two very difficult questions by collectors
and lovers of ceramics – when is a teapot not a teapot and
how is it correct to say that the many strange shapes of the
early eighteenth century are superb works of art, whereas
great collectors and ceramic experts are often very scornful
of copies of the same shapes made by Victorian potters?

To answer the first question: any practical object, be it
tea or coffee pot, jug or saucepan, motor car or aeroplane,
has to be of a particular shape to make it functional. It is no
good making a beautiful looking teapot that will not pour,
and there is no doubt that the best pouring shape is a
globular one. The globular, or round bodied pot has the
functional ability to channel the liquid in a smooth stream
towards the spout and combined with the fact that potters
find it the most satisfying shape to look at as well as being
basically easier than oval or square pots to make and fire,
this explains why so many globular pots have been made.
So while a teapot does not have to be of any particular
shape as long as it is practical, it is, obviously a bonus if it is
aesthetically pleasing as well.

As for the second question, the praising of an eighteenth
century shape and the running down of a Victorian close
copy: the potters of the early Georgian period seem to have
had a natural sense of taste and a fine feeling for the
material, which the Victorians with a few exceptions did
not possess. When the Georgians produced a vessel in the
form of an animal, or a handle in the shape of a twig, it was
always treated in pure ceramic terms, whereas the Victorians had the annoying habit of trying to make the body
look like another material, unjustified in pure ceramic
terms. To put it in another way, a Georgian twig handle
would look ceramic, the Victorian like a twig. Now this
was very clever of the Victorians, of course, but it does not

necessarily make artistic sense to make one material look like another. The Victorians often lost sight of the clay in contrast to the single minded approach of the Georgians. It is all a matter of feeling.

Although the round teapot was to become the most common shape, it had its rivals in cylindrical and other forms. The drawings on page 65 show the main developments of the three broad types of shapes – round, cylindrical and oval and other types. Set out in this way it is interesting to see that all three types ran concurrently in the second half of the eighteenth century, although only oval and elongated shapes survived into the nineteenth century. A revival of the round pot, albeit with Victorian 'knobs' on it in the form of elaborate handle, spout, foot and cover, came back in about 1840, which has continued to the present day.

After the Elers type of teapot of about 1700, European pots made a slow but steady movement away from Oriental shapes, although many of the shapes of the early eighteenth century have echoes of the Chinese. However the styles began to show gradual use of a Europeanised Orientalism, what is most usefully termed Chinoiserie, by which is meant an Oriental influence expressed in a European way.

This Chinoiserie is to be seen strongly in salt glazed and Astbury-wares of Staffordshire, the fine early Meissen porcelain wares and the first English artificial, or soft paste, porcelains, especially those of Worcester, although some English factories could produce quite strange Oriental shapes as late as the 1750's. Decorations could be of three types, copies of Chinese and Japanese, Chinoiseries or European. All these styles can well be seen in the teapots of Worcester, certainly the most successful English eighteenth century factory in producing consistently fine teapots.

English earthenware teapots of the 1740's are epitomised by the many experiments done by Josiah Wedgwood during his work with Thomas Whieldon, especially with regard to the pineapple and cauliflower shapes, tortoise-shell and solid agate colours which are the most easily recognised Wedgwood/Whieldon effects. Also produced by this partnership were black iron-glazed wares (often called 'Jackfield' after the village in Shropshire where similar black glazed wares were produced) and green copper-glazed earthenwares, many of these having echoes of the

Plate **64**
Very rare Chinese teapot and stand of the Ch'ien Lung period (1736–95), painted in England by J. H. O'Neale with the fable of the horse and the ass, the stand with the fox and grapes. Some Chinese porcelains were sent to London in the white for decorating. Teapots were usually sold with a stand, so that the hot base of the pot would not damage the table. Height 7½ in. *Shand Kydd Collection*

Plate **65**
Three fine early Chelsea porcelain teapots. Below, right, rare form of strawberry leaf modelling, finely painted with garden flowers. Left, an ovoid, fluted form painted with harbour scenes in the style of Meissen, *circa* 1752. Height 5 in. Above, a miniature in form of an acanthus leaf, decoration of flaming dragon, or 'Tyger' pattern. Mark, impressed triangle, *circa* 1740–45. Height 4 in. *Shand Kydd Collection*

Plate **66**
Pair of early Chelsea teapots in form of a Chinese god sitting on a cushion, holding a serpent which forms the spout; a branch forms the handle, curving round the pot and terminating at the top. This is the only known pair of these pots in a collection.
Shand Kydd Collection (acknowledgement to Frank Tilley, FRSA)

typical applied ornament used by Elers, thin wafers of scrolls produced from metal dies. These experiments stood Wedgwood in good stead when he started his own factory, especially influencing his preoccupation with effects resembling natural stones.

The influence of silver vessels on English shapes was very great at first (plate 10) but by the 1760's pure ceramic shapes had taken over. Other great influences to make their marks were rococo (plate 16) and neoclassicism.

Neoclassicism, inspired by the architecture of Robert Adam and breathing something of Roman forms found at Pompeii and Herculaneum exerted a great influence upon English silversmiths and potters and is to be seen at its finest in the teapots of Josiah Wedgwood, either in the basalts and jaspers or in the new Queens Ware or cream-ware bodies. Creamware did fair to rival porcelain in the last quarter of the eighteenth century, although bone china, claimed as the invention of Josiah Spode, by the end of the century, won back the public's favour for translucent wares.

The new century saw bone china in England and porcelain in Europe as the main material for teawares for the more wealthy and an oval shape established as the main form. Cheaper wares were still made in basalts, creamwares or the so-called ironstone, stone china or semi-porcelain bodies, none of these being the expensive bone china body using oxbone as its main constituent but a cheaper vitrified earthenware.

Patterns in the early nineteenth century could range from the splendidly hand painted scenes, floral subjects, shells and feathers of Worcester, Derby, Swansea and Nantgarw or the great Continental factories to the blue prints of Staffordshire. The invention of transfer printing on porcelain, first used superbly well at Worcester, could sometimes descend to the lowest depths in the cheapest wares of the nineteenth century.

The teapot was becoming a familar object in the homes of the poorer classes; with the lowering of the cost of tea the beverage had become the popular drink. Not for the poor the use of finest bone china or beautifully hand painted porcelain, for them the use of crude earthenwares, simple cheap lustrewares from Staffordshire or similar Potteries areas in other parts of the world.

Most of the teapots of the first half of the nineteenth

Plate **67**
Chelsea red anchor period teapot painted with a fable from Aesop by J. H. O'Neale, reverse with flowers. Aesop's fables were favourite subjects of O'Neale and this one is admirably adapted to the fine shape of the pot. Height $6\frac{1}{4}$ in., *circa* 1750.
Shand Kydd Collection (acknowledgement to Frank Tilley, FRSA)

century were of elongated shapes. These could vary from square, possibly with flutes at the side (Coalport or New-hall), to long, oval, boat shapes with high prows at the front into which the covers slotted. By 1840 the styles of pots had begun to look Victorian, with elaborately boisterous handles and spouts and often curving feet. Many of the ceramic pots tended to ape the European silver vessels of a few years earlier. At this time the round shape began to reappear, although the handles and spouts can be so complicated that it is a little difficult to recognise the basic roundness.

Oval and round shapes continued to battle with each other into the 1860's but the most important influence of the middle Victorian period was the rediscovery of Japanese forms. For many centuries the Japanese had divorced themselves from European influences, although the West had imitated whatever Japanese styles they could obtain. So we see the lovely Kakiemon and Arita copying at Worcester and Bow in the 1760's, the Imari patterns (the so-called 'Japans') of Worcester, Derby and Spode of 1810's and then the Japanesque of 1780's.

This fifty or sixty year cycle of interest in Japanese ceramic arts is very interesting and if it had not been for the last world war there is little doubt in my mind that we would have had the next sequence of the cycle in the 1940's.

The Japanese first exhibited in Europe at the London Exhibition of 1862 and the forms and patterns took the West by storm. Red stonewares of a traditional style of the 1600's and modernistic shapes which were square or diamond in form with Japanesque patterns of prunus, bamboos, small animals and butterflies, poured out of European factories, under the leadership of Worcester. Everyone went Japanese mad for a few years.

There were many curious teapots produced in the last quarter of the nineteenth century, some, like the comical 'Aesthetic' teapot (plate 149) or Royle's self pouring pot (plate 150) having great liveliness about them.

A great number of teapots were produced that were probably not meant to be used, such as the huge quantity made by German and Austrian firms and by such English companies as Goss (plate 154). These were made for tourists and trippers to the English seaside and as fairings, that is gifts bought or worn at fairs.

Possibly the boldest shape of the Victorians is the 'Barge'

Plate **68** *(above)*
Longton Hall teapot in the form of a globe artichoke with rows of green leaves springing from the base. Although admittedly a comical curiousity it has tremendous spirit and style. Height 6½ in., *circa* 1755–7.
Shand Kydd Collection (acknowledgement to Frank Tilley, FRSA)

Plate **70** *(centre right)*
Two contrasting Bow porcelain teapots. Left, a rare but typical early form, decorated with sprigged prunus or plum blossom. Height 4¾ in., *circa* 1750. Right, a later globular pot with Chinese type spout painted with crude Chinoiseries in underglaze blue of typical Bow blurred type. Height 5¾ in. *circa* 1752–5.
Shand Kydd Collection (acknowledgement to Frank Tilley, FRSA)

Plate 69
Longton Hall teapot with moulded tulip petals on the base, neck and cover. The handle twists around the foot forming the base and then runs up to the green scroll spout which it joins, giving a fine sense of unity to a pot, which could so easily have been chaotic. Height 4½ in., *circa* 1755.
Shand Kydd Collection (acknowledgement to Frank Tilley, FRSA)

Plate 71
Bow teapot of simple, but pleasing, barrel shape, well proportioned and a complete contrast to the more flamboyant shapes of its Chelsea neighbour. Height 4 in., *circa* 1755.
Victoria and Albert Museum

teapot (plate 152) with the typical so called 'Rockingham' glaze, a lustrous dark brown colour that really has no connection with Rockingham but was produced in Staffordshire and a number of other places in England.

Most of these curious shapes, of course, were not really meant for use; the pots for ordinary use being of a simple plain round shape, with sparse decoration, typical of the wares sent to Canada (plate 148) or those made in that country (plate 146). At the very bottom of the social scale came the simple, large, brown glazed teapot, often called a 'brown Betty', devoid of decoration and purely functional.

Such shapes take us into the present century, where in the first fifty years hardly any new shapes made their appearance, most of them having a sturdy round brown Betty appearance of a rather simpering Victorian prettiness. The post-war years have seen many attempts to produce new and improved shapes, with a continuation of the great battle between round and oval.

The last photographs in the book are of the prize winners in a competition to design a new teapot, organised by the Tea Council and Josiah Wedgwood and Sons Ltd. The competition was open to students attending a full time course in design and the brief was 'to design a perfect teapot, one that combines function and beauty for production in fine bone china or earthenware', decoration not being required but only shape.

The three winning teapots most interestingly exhibit the three main competing forms shown on page 65, the prize-winning pot being of round form, the second of oval shape and the third cylindrical. It is also interesting that the first prize was awarded to the design which was of traditional design, looking not unlike an early stoneware shape of the year 1700.

The adjudicators reported that the pot was well rounded, comfortable to hold, had good pouring qualities and a pleasant easy to grip lid; the lid is certainly an improvement on those of the seventeenth and eighteenth century which usually fell off in use, the biggest drawback in the function of early round bodied teapots.

It will be realised that all ceramic problems have been come across at some time or other and nothing is new under the sun. Even tea making machines are not new, the idea being seen on page 97 from the early nineteenth century, in this case for making coffee.

Plate **72**
'Landscape' teapot of unusual form, lobed body modelled in high relief by William Greatbach during the Whieldon/Wedgwood period with sheep and cattle in pasture, swans, man in a boat and trees, mottled colours on a cream ground. Height $4\frac{3}{4}$ in., *circa* 1760. *Harriet Carlton Goldweitz Collection*

Plate **73** *(right)*
Littler/Wedgwood teapot, saltglaze stoneware covered with blue cobalt glaze resembling lapis lazuli; such glaze attributed to William Littler of Longton Hall, who was brother-in-law to Aaron Wedgwood. Height 4 in., *circa* 1750.
Harriet Carlton Goldweitz Collection

Plate **74** *(far right)*
Whieldon/Wedgwood teapot with a beautiful marbled effect of glazing, *circa* 1755–58.
Wedgwood

Plate **75**
Two Wedgwood lead glazed earthenware teapots in the shape of a pineapple and a melon, green and yellow glazed to resemble the fruit. Heights $3\frac{1}{2}$ in. and $5\frac{1}{4}$ in., *circa* 1755–60.
Harriet Carlton Goldweitz Collection

Plate **76**
Two eighteenth century teapots, above Worcester, below Chinese, showing the basic differences in formation of handle and spout and proportions of body. The Worcester pot is outline printed and filled in, the Chinese one is painted.
Dyson Perrins Museum

	ROUND SHAPES	CYLINDRICAL SHAPES	NON-ROUND SHAPES
1700	ELERS		
1710	SALTGLAZE		
1720	MEISSEN		
1730	ASTBURY		
1740	SALTGLAZE	RED STONEWARE	SALTGLAZE
1750	JACKFIELD	SALTGLAZE	SALTGLAZE
1760	WORCESTER	WORCESTER	EARTHENWARE
1770	WORCESTER	WORCESTER	
1780	CREAMWARE	LEEDS	WORCESTER (CHAMBERLAIN)
1790	SEVRES HARD PASTE	PARIS	COALPORT BASALT
1800			NEWHALL
1810			WORCESTER
1820			NEWHALL
1830			SPODE
1840	ROCKINGHAM		STAFFORDSHIRE

Plate **77**
Wedgwood blue and white Jasper teapot, ornamented with figures from the subject 'Domestic Employment'. Designed by Lady Templeton and modelled by William Hackwood, marked 'Wedgwood'. 1783.
Wedgwood

COFFEE POTS

The earliest vessels used for pouring tea and coffee (or, for that matter, chocolate) were not greatly differentiated in Europe. The earliest coffee pots derived from the proto-types developed in the countries where the drinks originated and from materials natural to those countries; for example, porcelain in China and Japan, brass in the Near East and gourds in South America.

In Europe the earliest pots were made of silver, having a tapering round shape with a flat base and C-scroll handle set at a right angle to the tubular spout. The pouring was done by turning the wrist to the left.

The coffee pot has continued this basic tall shape ever since, as will be seen on page 71, teapots becoming squat and chocolate pots developing pierced covers so that stirring rods could be inserted. For many years both coffee pots and chocolate pots could have side handles, although many coffee pots had the present day normal idea of the handle in line with the spout. This duality continued to about 1725, from which time only chocolate pots had side handles.

With regard to the positioning of the spouts there is really no reason why those of coffee pots should come from the bottom, while those of teapots emerge from half way up the vessel. By tradition the coffee pot has remained a graceful tall shape, especially in England (plate 110) although the earliest Continental porcelain pots tended to be of jug-like shape (plate 89).

The development of the tall coffee pot shape was very slow and hesitant. For many years the only change in the shape of silver coffee pots was the replacement of the plain spout by a more gracefully curving swan neck shape about 1670. By 1680 handles and spouts had grown even longer and more graceful and at the end of the seventeenth century they were mounted just below the middle point of the body.

Through the William and Mary period, the basic shape remained a truncated cone, the flat bottom standing firmly on the table giving the shape a severity of form calling to mind the plainness of silver of the Commonwealth period. The reign of Queen Anne, however, under the influence of the Huguenot silversmiths, saw many bold experiments in design and ornament.

The most important change in shape was from a round to

Plate **78**
Wedgwood 'Three Coloured Jasper' teapot. Cylindrical shape, applied decoration in relief, of acanthus leaf, swags and medallions of classical figures, the white, green and lilac producing a rare and sought-after combination, marked 'Wedgwood'. Height $3\frac{1}{2}$ in., *circa* 1800.
Harriet Carlton Goldweitz Collection

a basically octagonal shape. This not only affected the pot itself but also the cover, which had to change from a flaring cone into an octagonal dome. The base was also made smaller which greatly accentuated the upward sweep of the shape.

Pear shaped forms began to vie with the truncated cone shape in England and the earliest pottery shapes began to copy both examples, as did English porcelain when the material was discovered.

Decoration at first was not important on coffee pots and ranged from the so-called cut card ornament of the William and Mary period, which resembled serrated leaves at the base of spouts, handle sockets and the handle grip, to a simply engraved Chinoiserie. In the periods of Queen Anne and George I the decoration was even plainer in silver. The only excitement was found in the decorations on German porcelain and the occasional English earthenware pots, although ceramic coffee pots have always been relatively little made in comparison with silver.

In the reign of George II, ornate decorations began to be used, under the influence of the French. The use of trellis, portrait heads and, in particular scallop shells, were common. Of these silver patterns the most popular used on ceramics were shells, which revived in interest at the end of the eighteenth century.

The more fantastic decorations on silver vessels, for example those of Paul de Lamerie, did not have their counterpart ceramically, although Chelsea, in particular, moved heavily into the field of English rococo. This stemmed from an absorption of the French motives of Louis XV, elaborate uses of scrolls, shells, spirals, rockwork and masks from the 1740's. Rococo passed many English factories by, some, such as Worcester, ignoring it almost completely, preferring to base their coffee pots upon earlier and plainer silver shapes, either the cone or the pear form.

The reign of George III, after continuing to flirt with an even more elaborate rococo, made a dramatic change into what might be thought of as the better taste of the neoclassicism of Robert Adam style, based upon classical elements of ancient Rome. Coffee pots could appear in a shape formed of two equal zones, rather like an Adams urn, typified by some of the shapes produced by Wedgwood.

From 1800 very few coffee pots were produced in

Plate **79**
Worcester coffee pot, embossed 'feather' moulding, transfer printed in onglaze black with a Chinoiserie subject either side and butterflies. Height 9 in., *circa* 1758–60.
Dyson Perrins Museum

ceramics, metal being the commonly used material. In
fact, from about 1780, ceramic coffee pots are very rare and
it is not until the present century that the shape returns,
many factories never making the form, for example
Nantgarw and Swansea.

The present day shapes can be of pear shape form,
either of eighteenth century form like a pear with its
larger half at the bottom or the same form turned upside
down, which first started in about 1840, as shown on page
71. Or else the coffee pot can be made to complement the
shape of the teapot in a range which all have to have the
same basic shape imposed upon them, be they tea cup,
milk jug, teapot or coffee pot. This is often a very difficult
thing to do and the imposition of a unified design over a
range of different shapes for the tea and coffee table can
sometimes produce weirdly uncomfortable shapes that
are neither one thing nor another.

However, the best designed modern shapes of coffee
pots often have more excitement than similar teapots and
any collections which do not include good present day
examples cannot be called complete.

VIENNA 1725   MEISSEN 1730   WEDGWOOD/LITTLER 1750   BOW 1755

LIVERPOOL 1760   WORCESTER 1760   DERBY 1770   WORCESTER 1770

WEDGWOOD 1777   TURNER 1780   TURNER 1790   TURNER 1800

WEDGWOOD 1805-10   LE NOVE 1815   NEWHALL 1815   SPODE 1840

Plate **81** *(left)*
Fine Worcester porcelain teapot of late silver type modelling on a round shape, painted in enamels with a copy of a Chinese subject. The beautiful proportions, fine decoration, a body and glaze that did not crack when boiling liquids were put in, explain why Worcester teawares were so keenly appreciated in the eighteenth century. Height 5½ in., *circa* 1760.
Sotheby and Co.

Plate **82** *(below left)*
Worcester teapot, vertically fluted painted in onglaze colours with two groups of figures in garden scenes and detached sprays in Oriental style. Height 6 in., *circa* 1755.
Dyson Perrins Museum

Plate **83** *(above right)*
Worcester teapot of silver style, squat octagonal form with embossed panels divided into three parts painted in underglaze blue with Chinoiserie subjects. Height 5 in. A painter's mark under base, *circa* 1755.
Dyson Perrins Museum

Plate **84** *(centre right)*
Worcester teapot, vertically lobed, printed in onglaze black outline and filled in and tinted in colours, pattern called 'Red Bull', painted formal borders in red, green and black. Height 5 in., *circa* 1758.
Dyson Perrins Museum

Plate **85** *(right)*
An unusual Worcester teapot form, a combination of two equal cone shapes, painted in underglaze blue with the 'Mansfield' pattern. *Circa* 1758–60.
Shand Kydd Collection (acknowledgement to Frank Tilley, FRSA)

Plate **86** *(above)*
Two contrasting Worcester
teapots. Left, round shape, painted
with a copy of a Chinese subject.
Right, a taller round shape with
flower knob, transfer printed in
outline and coloured in by hand
with the 'Red Bull' pattern. Height
$4\frac{3}{4}$ in.
Sotheby and Co.

Plate **87** *(centre left)*
Rare Worcester teapot,
barrel-shaped with two lateral
reeded bands coloured yellow.
Between bands, floral sprays in the
Oriental style. Height 4 in., *circa*
1760.
Dyson Perrins Museum

Plate **88** *(below left)*
Worcester teapot of cylindrical
shape with sharply sloping
shoulders painted in the manner of
the Japanese. Height 5 in., *circa*
1760.
Dyson Perrins Museum

Plate **89**
Meissen coffee pot, painted with a
Chinoiserie scene by J. G.
Heroldt; the handle is
characteristic of Meissen. *Circa*
1720.
Winifred Williams

Plate **90**
Rare and very beautiful small-sized
Worcester coffee pot of globular
shape, rare yellow ground,
reserving panels of flower sprays
painted in onglaze colours with
gilding, sprays on the ground.
Height 5½ in., *circa* 1765.
Dyson Perrins Museum

Plate **91**
Attractive Worcester coffee pot,
moulded with chrysanthemum
pattern, painted in underglaze
blue with a stylised
chrysanthemum leaf pattern.
Height 9 in. Mark, a painted open
crescent, *circa* 1770.
Dyson Perrins Museum

Plate **92**
Worcester teapot of beautiful
proportions decorated underglaze
with powder blue (cobalt blown
on in powder form resulting in a
speckled appearance) reserving fan
shaped and circular reserves
painted with cobalt oxide. Height
5½ in. Mark, open crescent and
fretted square (usually found on
this pattern), *circa* 1770.
Dyson Perrins Museum

Plate **93** *(below)*
Superb Worcester teapot, pierced
handle and moulded spout,
underglaze scale blue, reserving
panels of flowering
chrysanthemums in Oriental style.
Height 5¼ in. Mark, a fretted
square, *circa* 1765.
Dyson Perrins Museum

Plate 94 *(left)*
Capo di Monte part tea service, beautifully painted with butterflies and insects probably by Giovanni Caselli. Height of teapot 5¾ in. Mark, blue *fleur de lys. Circa* 1750.
Christie Manson and Woods

Plate 95 *(below left)*
A remarkable Meissen tea and coffee service, possibly the most complete of its kind, even having matching porcelain spoons; superbly controlled yellow ground (Meissen was most skilful at this difficult colour) reserving panels painted probably by C. F. Heroldt. Height of teapot 6 in., marked with blue crossed swords and the same gilt letter under the base and cover (a guarantee that the cover belongs). *Circa* 1740–45.
Christie Manson and Woods

Plate 96 *(above right)*
Attractive Liverpool teapot (probably Wolfe's factory) with typical double linking handle, enamel painted in pink, green and blue. Height 6 in., *circa* 1790.
Dyson Perrins Museum

Plate 97 *(right)*
Liverpool teapot from Richard Chaffer's factory, transfer printed in onglaze enamels by Sadler and Green of Liverpool; both shape and decoration copying Worcester but not doing it quite as well.
City of Liverpool Museums

79

Plate **98**
Teapot and teapoy from Philip
Christian's factory in Liverpool.
The shape basically copies
Worcester but does not achieve the
superb proportions of handle and
spout of the original. Height
$4\frac{7}{8}$ in. *Circa* 1765.
City of Liverpool Museums

Plate **99**
Lowestoft teapot, painted by the
'Tulip' painter in typical tones of
purple, orange and green, orange
panels around handle and spout.
While Lowestoft does not have
quite the assurance and balance of
Worcester, this pot is a very good
specimen. Height 6 in., *circa* 1780.
Dyson Perrins Museum

Plate **100**
Bristol (Champion's factory) hard
paste porcelain teapot and stand
from a service made for Mark
Harford. Decoration includes
panels of landscapes; the shape is
highly characteristic of Bristol.
Height $5\frac{1}{2}$ in., stand $5\frac{1}{2}$ in. width.
Circa 1775.
Shand Kydd Collection

Plate **101**
Liverpool 'punch' pot from
Pennington's factory. Moulded
panels have Chinoiseries subjects,
borders of pink scale top and
bottom and elaborate cell border.
These very large pots, especially
if they have no straining holes, are
often referred to as punch pots.
Height 10 in., *circa* 1780.
Shand Kydd Collection
(acknowledgement to Frank Tilley,
FRSA)

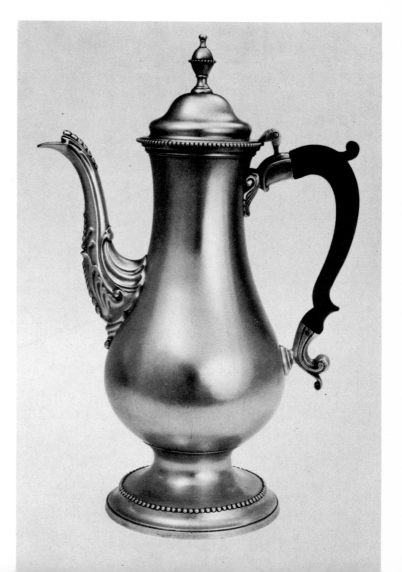

Plate **102**
Exceptionally large-sized coffee
pot made in silver by Charles
Wright. Height 13¾ in. 1774.
Folger Coffee Company collection.
Courtesy of the Procter and
Gamble Co.

Plate **103**
Wedgwood creamware teapot
enamelled in puce, red, black,
yellow and green by David
Rhodes with horizontal and
diagonal bands of florets and
chevrons, leaf moulded handle and
spout. Height 5¾ in., *circa* 1775.
Phillips Son and Neale

Plate **104** *(below)*
Three Leeds creamware teapots
showing two typical handle and
knob forms, the only known set of
prodigal son parable scenes by
Greatbach transfer printed in
black and coloured in enamels;
scenes are flanked by powder blue
panels with iron-red flowers.
Height 5½ in., *circa* 1772–5.
*Shand Kydd Collection
(acknowledgement to Frank Tilley,
FRSA)*

Plate **105**
Early creamware teapot, probably
Wedgwood, deep cream colour,
cabbage spout, pierced ogee shape
knob, partially glazed base, traces
of saffron in glaze, transfer
printed in black with 'Battledore
and Shuttlecock', landscape on
reverse. Height 5 in., *circa* 1760.
Harriet Carlton Goldweitz Collection

Plate **106**
Creamware teapot, probably
Leeds, globular shape, light cream
body, ribbed spout with moulded
acanthus leaf, beautiful rope-twist
entwined handle with moulded
flower terminals, transfer printed
in deep burgundy with 'Tea
Party' and on reverse 'The
Shepherd', floral knob. Height
4¼ in., *circa* 1775.
Harriet Carlton Goldweitz Collection

Collections and Collectors

There remains to say a few words about forming a collection of tea and coffee pots.

I have known a great number of collectors of ceramics and virtually all of them include some tea and coffee pots among their collections, usually as part of other shapes and objects. Thus a teapot will be arranged with its attendant cups and saucers, milk jug and sugar basin, slop basin, cake plate and spoon tray, looking like the king surrounded by his courtiers. Or a coffee pot will be used on a shelf to break up the line of other shapes, to give height and dramatic contrast to a group of plates, cups and saucers.

There are, however, collectors who specialise in teapots and coffee pots only, recognising in these shapes the supreme challenge to the skill of the potter – the necessity to produce both practicability and aesthetic beauty in the same vessel. I know many of these and a visit to their collections can be an uplifting experience. Whether the pots are arranged in cabinets, or on open shelves, or as an architectural frieze right around a room at eye level, along a hall, or running up the stairs, such displays can be a thrilling sight.

Many of these collections have become world famous. Who has not heard of the Shand Kydd teapot collection, every pot a superb piece and many of them are illustrated in this book. Another and much more recent collection is that formed by Mrs. Harriet Carlton Goldweitz and this again is not just an assembly of as many pots as can be bought, but everyone is a choice piece, specially chosen to cover some particular aspect.

Let me not hide the fact, that such collections would cost a considerable amount of money to form, some rare teapots fetching several thousand pounds at auction, but do not let this put you off. Most interesting collections can be formed for relatively little money if the collector is not

Plate **107**
Wedgwood Queens Ware coffee pot, transfer printed with a rural scene. *Circa* 1775.
Wedgwood

Plate **108** *(far right)*
Meissen lime green ground coffee
pot with panels painted by J. G.
Heintze; the handle is a
characteristic Meissen shape of this
period.
Circa 1740.
Winifred Williams

put off by some damage to the pot or is prepared to explore
fields that are not at present in vogue, a number of which
are shown in this book. Damage is not regarded in such a
bad light as once it was but a pot with chips or cracks,
knob or cover missing, should cost very much less than a
perfect one. You must not expect, however, to have the
reasonable certainty of selling such a damaged piece at a
profit, as should be the case with a well bought perfect
and fine pot.

Many magnificent collections have been formed of
damaged pots and typical of these is that of a man known to
all collectors as 'Teapot' Williams. Try to imagine the
pleasure he obtained from his great collection of many
hundreds of pots, mainly English porcelain and earthenware, formed over many years, a great number of which
were sold at a dispersal sale in the London salerooms of
Phillips some years ago. Perhaps one day a reader of this
book will acquire one of these pots and, I hope, love it as
much as did its original owner.

Plate **109**
Beautiful early Worcester coffee
pot of finely proportioned silver
shape, exquisitely painted with
flowers in a mixture of Chinese
and Dutch style. *Circa* 1751–4.
Winifred Williams

Although there are many great collectors of teapots,
there are relatively few who collect coffee pots alone and
yet the latter can be much more exciting and dramatic, as I
hope the photographs in this book will show.

It must be realised, however, that ceramic coffee pots
are much rarer than ceramic teapots. In the 1760's and 70's
no self respecting tea service would be made without its
coffee pot, although the coffee cup had to share the same
saucer as the tea cup. It was sensibly reasoned that tea and
coffee were not drunk at the same time, so cost would be
reduced by having, say, twelve teacups (or bowls), twelve
saucers and six coffee cups in your service. To this would
be added milk (or cream) jug, sugar basin (with cover),
slop basin, cake plates, spoon tray, teapot and stand, and
coffee pot.

There were no small bread and butter plates at this period
(they did not arrive until the mid Victorian period) as tea
was not a sit-down meal at a table but was taken sitting
casually around in chairs, cake being passed around on a
cake plate. By 1800 few coffee pots were being made in
ceramics, most of those in use being made of silver, which
material was ever threatening to take teapots over.

A collection could be built up on a single theme, such as
all the examples being of one factory, country or period.
This can make for a unified whole, although the danger is

Plate **110** *(right)*
Superb Worcester coffee pot,
underglaze scale blue ground
(the scales hand painted in cobalt
oxide) reserving panels painted
with fabulous birds, outlined with
fine gilding; Dr. Wall period.
Mark, a fretted square. *Circa* 1770.
Dr. Riley Collection

86

that an unwary collector will acquire every possible pot within the laid down scope of his collection irrespective of quality. With this proviso, some suggestions are saltglaze, creamwares, Worcester, Wedgwood, English porcelain, Staffordshire eighteenth or nineteenth centuries, blue printed wares, Victorian or craftsmen potters.

Interesting collections could be built up comparing one factory or period with another, Chinese with European, porcelain with pottery, ceramics with silver. Never be frightened of thinning out your collection nor of replacing a poor example by a better one; the advantages of doing this are many, for example in improving the quality of the collection and in the paying for a new piece by selling off an old one, the aim being the development of the whole. Learn to back your own judgment against that of a dealer or other collectors, not being too greatly worried about which factory a piece came from but looking more at its inherent qualities.

Whatever type of collection you form, or even if you only treat the pots as part of your collection, it is hoped that this book will have led you to look at coffee and teapots in a different light.

Plate **111**
Fine Wedgwood Black Basalt teapot of boat shape, painted in encaustic colours and anticipating the oval shapes of the turn of the century. *Circa* 1788. *Wedgwood*

Plate **112**
Rare creamware teapot and cover
with cylindrical body covered with
a mottled manganese glaze
splashed with green. The double
twisted handle terminates in
flowerheads suggesting a Leeds
origin, but the pot may be
Melbourne. Height 4 in., late
eighteenth century.
*Private Collection
(acknowledgement to Tilley and Co.)*

Plate **113**
Two Wedgwood Queens Ware, or
creamware, teapots. Left, transfer
printed with the death of General
Wolfe, *circa* 1780. Right, hand
painted Chinoiseries, with double
twist handle, very like those used
by Leeds, *circa* 1770.
Wedgwood

Plate **114** *(far left)*
Leeds creamware coffee pot of very slender and graceful proportions, pear shaped body with ribbed and beaded borders, acanthus leaves at base of spout, typical entwined strap handles, vertical stripes of brilliant green glaze. Height 8 in., *circa* 1770.
Harriet Carlton Goldweitz Collection

Plate **115** *(left)*
Leeds 'Pearlware' teapot, cylindrical shape with strap handle, body covered with light blue dip, border in black and white checkered dip, good example of the attractive pearlwares. Height $4\frac{3}{8}$ in., *circa* 1810.
Harriet Carlton Goldweitz Collection

Plate **116** *(below left)*
Beautiful Derby teapot with typical yellow ground reserving landscape panel, named under the base as 'Near Forfar Scotland'. Normal crown above X and D mark and pattern number 531. Early nineteenth century.
Ian Henderson Collection

Plate **117** *(above)*
Curious Staffordshire 'Othello' teapot, modelled by John Voyez, said to have been made by Ralph Wood. Height $8\frac{1}{2}$ in., *circa* 1775.
Stoke-on-Trent City Museum

Plate **118**
Chamberlain's Worcester teapot of oval form, painted and gilded with 'Blue Lily' pattern, popular at both Flight and Barr's factory at Worcester and at Caughley. Height $6\frac{1}{4}$ in. Mark inside the cover (a favourite place to hide) 'Chamberlains Worcester', *circa* 1795.
Dyson Perrins Museum

Plate 119 *(left)*
A range of typical Wedgwood teapots. Top left, Queens Ware shell edge, traces of oil gilding, *circa* 1775. Top right, Queen's ware, chrysanthemum pattern, early nineteenth century. Centre, bone china, painted English landscape scenes, gold line, *circa* 1815. Below left, china, oval parapet shape, *circa* 1814. Right, cauliflower teapot, *circa* 1755. In front, cane coloured, *circa* 1830.
Wedgwood

Plate 120 *(below left)*
Four Worcester pots from the Flight factory of the period 1800–15. Top left, oval, scalloped top, painted purple and green spotted 'pheasant eye' diaper, length $9\frac{5}{8}$ in. Mark B and X incised, *circa* 1800. Top right, coffee pot of narrow, flattened, galleon shape, salmon ground and gilding. Height $8\frac{3}{4}$ in., *circa* 1803. Below left, teapot on its stand, boat shaped, salmon bands and gilding, length 10 in. Mark F B B under a crown impressed, *circa* 1815. Below right, oval, stepped shape near base, red and brown imbricated border. Height 7 in. Mark incised 'B', *circa* 1800.
Dyson Perrins Museum

Plate 121 *(above right)*
Group of teapots of around 1800 in date. From left, top row, Castleford, Coalport, Worcester. Middle row, Coalport, Newhall. Last row, Worcester (Flight and Barr), Worcester (Flight and Barr) and Worcester (Chamberlain).
Dyson Perrins Museum and Neal French Collection

Plate 122 *(centre right)*
Nice group of porcelain tewares from the Newhall factory of Stoke-on-Trent. This shape was made by several English factories but none achieved the superb form and balance of the original. Height of teapot $4\frac{1}{2}$ in., *circa* 1795.
Stoke-on-Trent City Museum

Plate 123 *(right)*
Newhall teapot and stand with typically rather crude Chinoiserie decoration. Teapot height 6 in., length $9\frac{1}{2}$ in., stand length 8 in. *Circa* 1805.
Stoke-on-Trent City Museum

Plate **124** *(left)*
Yellow canary lustre teapot, transfer printed in black with a tea party subject, cover fitting well into the oval boat shaped form; probably Sewell Pottery, Newcastle. Height 5 in., *circa* 1810.
Harriet Carlton Goldweitz Collection

Plate **125** *(below)*
Swansea pottery coffee pots. Top a miniature, painted in enamels, height 5¾ in. Below, both printed in blue with Chinoiserie subjects, height 9¾ in.
Sir Leslie Joseph Collection

Plate **126** *(right)*
Top, Glamorgan pottery teapot, transfer printed in black with rustic scenes. Height 5⅞ in. Mark 'Opaque China' and 'B B & I' in scrolls, and figure 4 printed in black, '6' impressed. Below, Swansea, Dyfatty Street, pottery teapot, elaborate three scroll handle, so called 'Rockingham' glaze. Height 6½ in. Mark '6' impressed.
Sir Leslie Joseph Collection

Plate **127**
Nantgarw teapot, cover and stand
of typical shape, the decoration all
in gold of wheatear and grapevine.
Mark under the stand 'Nantgarw
CW' impressed.
W. D. John Collection

Plate **128** *(above right)*
George IV Sheffield plate coffee
maker. The funnel is a coffee
caddy – from where the ground
coffee is spooned on to a perforated
plate in the cylinder at the opposite
end. The centre boiler is filled with
water which, when boiled, passes
through the curved tube into the
large cylinder where it drips
through the coffee into the lower
compartment and can be drawn
off through the tap. Height 19 in.,
length of base 18 in. *Circa* 1828.
Folger Coffee Company collection.
Courtesy of the Procter and
Gamble Co.

Plate **129** *(right)*
Silver teapot and cream jug, *circa*
1820.
Sotheby and Co.

Plate 130 *(left)*
Spode teapot of pleasing fluted oval form, printed decoration, early nineteenth century. Height 7 in.
Stoke-on-Trent City Museum

Plate 131 *(centre left)*
Davenport Pottery teapot of silver pattern, decorated with blue transfer prints of typical Staffordshire type. Mark, anchor and 'Davenport' printed in blue. *Circa* 1830.
Stoke-on-Trent City Museum

Plate 132 *(below left)*
Miles Mason teapot of typical and pleasing oval shape, transfer printed with willow pattern type scenes that followed on from the eighteenth-century Chinoiseries. Length 11 in., *circa* 1820.
Stoke-on-Trent City Museum

Plate 133 *(above right)*
Swansea porcelain teapots. Top, rare shape, with deep recess for cover, spout moulded with acanthus leaf, body and cover painted with band of poppy heads on a fawn ground. Pattern number 297. Height $5\frac{1}{8}$ in., length 7 in. Mark, 'Swansea' in red script. Below, silver shape, cover with pyramidal fluted knob, decorated with Japan pattern. Mark, '216' in red script (pattern number). Height $5\frac{1}{4}$ in., length $6\frac{3}{4}$ in. Both 'duck-egg' paste.
Sir Leslie Joseph Collection

Plate 134 *(above, far right)*
Nantgarw porcelain teapots. Top, round shape, cover with pyramidal knob, handle and spout with anthemion gilding. Height $5\frac{1}{8}$ in., length $6\frac{1}{4}$ in. Below, flattened globular shape, cone flower knob, recess for cover. Height $4\frac{1}{2}$ in. No marks.
Sir Leslie Joseph Collection

Plate 135 *(below right)*
Nantgarw porcelain teapot, cover and stand, superbly painted in enamel colours.
Diameter $8\frac{1}{2}$ in., *Circa* 1818–1820.
Collection of W. D. John

How Teapots and Coffee pots are made

Plate **136**
Most attractive Davenport boat shaped teapot, enamel painting in brown. Height 4 in., length 8½ in. Early nineteenth century. Mark, anchor and 'Davenport' impressed.
Stoke-on-Trent City Museum

Plate **137**
Pretty Grainger (Worcester) teapot, painted in tones of green and yellow and gilding, the shape pointing the way to the more extravagant Victorian shapes to come. Unmarked, like most early Grainger, but with pattern '214X' under the base, which corresponds with the factory pattern books. Height 7½ in., *circa* 1825–30.
Private Collection

I am sure it will be of interest to collectors to know something about how pots are produced. This will lead to greater understanding of why the pot appears as it does and explain many of the difficulties that potters have to overcome.

There are two basic ways by which the shape is produced – throwing on a wheel or making in a mould.

Throwing is perhaps the easiest method to comprehend, most people having seen a thrower at work. The process involves the throwing of a ball of clay on to a revolving wheel, the ball is then 'centred' by squeezing the two hands around the clay and squashing it to revolve centrally on the wheel, squeezing the ball upwards and pushing it downwards several times to get the clay into a good condition and then flattening it into a round cake spinning without a wobble. It is most important to centre the ball of clay perfectly as otherwise the resultant pot will not be of good shape nor will the walls of the vessel be of even thickness.

Into the centre of the flattened ball the potter presses his two thumbs to open up a hole, and then, using water as a lubricant on the wall, begins the 'throwing' – squeezing inwards and upwards with the two hands, one inside and one outside the pot. Almost as if by magic the sides of the vessel rise up into a cylindrical shape and several throws can be made, making the wall of the vessel thinner and the pot higher; then, or even during the throwing, the form of the body can be produced by exerting more pressure from the left, or inside, hand which causes the pot to curve outwards, or squeezing inwards to collar the rim.

When the form of the coffee pot or teapot has been completed, the pot is cut off the wheel with a wire. The pot is lifted off and put aside to dry somewhat into a condition known as 'green' or 'leather hard', a state somewhat like hard cheese. In this state it is put back upon a slowly revolving wheel and with a sharp turning tool, the surface

Plate 138
Typical continental late nineteenth century tourist teapot, transfer printed with Southampton Royal Pier, coloured by hand, with a cheap type of gold. Huge quantities of such tourist pieces were made in the period from 1860–1920 or so, much of it very poor quality, but this teapot is better than most.
Ian Henderson Collection

Plate 139
Two Japanese teabowls for the tea ceremony of typical form made by Toyozo Arakawa (born 1894) whose work was inspired by the pottery of the Momoyama Period.
Japan Information Centre

Plate 140
Beautiful modern stoneware teapot and bowl; the pot decorated with wax resist decoration between two glazes producing a particularly lovely effect; bowl with a 'Chun' glaze. Both fired at a temperature of 1,300°C in a reducing fire. Height of teapot 6 in. Made by Geoffrey Whiting, an English craftsman potter.

of the vessel is pared to remove the rings left during the throwing, to thin down the sides and generally to clean up the pot. Also at this stage the foot is 'turned', the surplus clay at the base is turned by an angled tool to make the footring on which the pot is to sit.

The potter at this stage also pierces the strainer holes through the pot and puts on the handle and the spout. These would generally be made by pressing the clay into two or more piece moulds and when the piece has been formed it is stuck on to the correct position on the pot, with liquid clay, known as slip. Covers and knobs are usually pressed in moulds, the knob being stuck on with slip. After thorough drying the pot is then ready for its first firing, known as the biscuit firing.

It is easy to understand that the only pots that can be made by this method are plain round or cylindrical shapes without any moulded decorations on the surface. It is, of course, possible to incise decoration into the surface or apply decoration, as in the form of sprigged flowers, sticking the pieces on with slip.

Any vessel with moulded decoration, or of oval, square or fluted shape, has to be made in a mould, either by pressing or slip casting. The oldest method is pressing, or to use the correct term when the clay is pressed into a re-volving mould – jolleying. By this method the clay is forced into the mould on which the pattern is incised. The resulting pot when it has dried and slightly contracted can be removed by opening up the parts of the mould and the surface of the pot will be impressed with the pattern from the mould.

All these above methods have used solid clay to produce the body of the pot, but one other important method used liquid clay, called slip. The process of slip casting is one that many collectors have great difficulty in comprehending but is really quite easy to understand.

Slip is poured into a plaster mould and forms a solid body on the inside of the mould as the water from the slip is absorbed by the porous plaster. When sufficient thickness has built up, the surplus slip is poured out; that is, the centre of the pot is poured away, leaving a hollow vessel. When the pot has dried out, after a short while, the mould is opened and the whole pot removed. This explains how a slip cast vessel can be hollow.

After casting, the foot will have to be turned out of the

solid clay at the base, or a separate foot shaped and pressed on to the bottom of the pot; also at this stage, the handle and spout are added, as on pressed or thrown pots.

By whichever method the pot has been made, it then has to have a sequence of kiln firings. Usually a pot has one firing at a high temperature to fuse the raw materials which shrink in size and become a body called 'biscuit'. Then the pot is dipped into raw glaze and fired again, in a lower firing to fuse the glaze on to the body. After this the enamel colours are put on the glaze and fused on to or into the glaze in one or more firings at lower temperatures still. Two or more decorating firings are usually necessary depending on the range of different colours used. Gold, being the lowest firing colour of all is fired last. The enamel colours are termed onglaze colours and no glaze is put over the top of them. The necessity to fire the glaze at temperatures over 1,000°C would burn away the enamel colours, which usually fire at temperatures between 700 and 800°C, these enamels being oxides of metals.

Some colours can withstand the fusing temperature of glaze and can be put on the biscuit with the glaze on top. Visualise the colour as the filling of a sandwich, the biscuit body and the glaze being the two slices of bread. The principle underglaze colour, as these are called, is cobalt, which produces blue. This is painted or printed on the biscuit body and the vessel can be glazed straight over the raw cobalt and fired, which may tend to make the highly volatile cobalt run and blur as in many Longton Hall and Bow pieces. Alternatively, the cobalt can be hardened on to the body in a separate firing before the raw glaze is applied, which helped the greater control of the blue as at Worcester.

If a pot has underglaze blue and onglaze enamels, as on the Worcester scale blue pieces, these are done in stages, the blue first under the glaze and then the enamels on top of the glaze in the reserve panels left white. Many differences in the effect of enamels can be seen between soft paste artificial porcelains and Chinese porcelains; in the former the colours usually sink deep into the softer glaze and body, giving a deeper, softer effect; in the latter the enamels remain hard and proud of the surface.

Some complicated glazes and bodies required special treatments. For instance in the case of delft, cobalt oxide had to be painted on to the raw tin glaze as the cobalt had

Plate 141 *(above)*
Spode teapot of moulded form, covered with a 'Rockingham' type glaze. Mark 'Spode' impressed. Height 7 in., *circa* 1845. *Stoke-on-Trent City Museum*

Plate 142 *(above right)*
Reproduction of an exquisite Worcester *dejeuner* service made for the Countess of Dudley in 1865; gold ground, applied droplets of turquoise and white enamels to simulate turquoise and pearls, painted classical heads in panels. Height of teapot 5¼ in. *Dyson Perrins Museum*

Plate 143
Grainger, Worcester teapot of basic oval shape with well designed and balanced shape almost ready to burst into the flamboyant Victorianism of the 1840's. Height 6¾ in. Mark 'G. Grainger, Royal Porcelain Works, Worcester', under a crown. *Circa* 1839. *Collection of Mrs. Marks, Worcestershire*

to fuse with the glaze. This meant that the painter could not rub out any bad painting, as he would remove some of the glaze as well. So delft tends to be very boldly, even crudely, painted, great delicacy being difficult and explains why the decoration is more boisterous than the careful painting on the hard surface of porcelain in the biscuit stage.

Decorations can be done in two main ways, painting or printing, or a combination of both. Painting is probably the easiest method to understand, being done with brushes of various sizes and shapes, but the ceramic painter has a number of problems to contend with that do not beset the canvas painter.

As previously explained, colours have to be fused into the body, often in sequences at different temperatures, paintings being built up in stages, especially for the more complicated landscapes. Another problem is that many colours undergo considerable changes during their firing in the kiln. A ceramic painter often has to put on colours that he knows are not the finished ones that he wants (unlike the painter on canvas) but that he hopes will become the correct ones on fusing in the kiln. This explains the frequent variation in colour between different pieces of a service.

Hand gilding is done in the same way, the skills of a fine gilder being as great as those of a painter, although collectors frequently concentrate more on the painting of a piece rather than the gilding. Fine gilding round a ceramic painting is rather like a superb frame around a canvas which can add lustre to the picture inside. The art of fine gilding is rather different from that of ceramic painting in that it needs slower and more careful work. Many people are amazed to learn how quickly many ceramic paintings are done, but the gilding can be a slow laborious task.

During the eighteenth century raw gold was mixed with honey as a medium to make the gold liquid, this being known as honey gilding. During the firing of the gold the honey burns away leaving the gold lightly fused on to the glaze and after burnishing (rubbing with silver sand) the gold appears a warm brown colour which, if looked at through a magnifying glass, is usually rather pitted and erupted.

From the nineteenth century the gold has been mixed

Plate **144**
Two Royal Worcester teapots of the Japanesque period, square or diamond shape, handles in form of lizards, decoration in Japanese style. Heights 6 in. and 8 in., *circa* 1875.
Dyson Perrins Museum

Plate **145**
Typical rather crude English
earthenware teapot of the
mid-nineteenth century. Such
pieces could have been made
almost anywhere, this one possibly
in Yorkshire. Height 9½ in.
Stoke-on-Trent City Museum

with oxide of mercury as a medium, known as mercuric oxide gilding, and this, after firing and burnishing, leaves a much harder, brighter, pure gold effect. This difference is important to bear in mind, as so many of the later nineteenth century copies of earlier pieces used mercuric instead of honey gilding and this is one very good way of telling later fakes.

I have, of course, been referring to the better qualities of gold used – twenty-two carat. The cheaper forms and various copper and other lustre effects, cannot be compared in quality with the finest gilded pieces and the differences can be easily appreciated by putting two teapots together – a finely gilded one of say the Barr Flight and Barr period of Worcester and a cheaper Staffordshire piece.

Coloured borders or grounds were usually painted on in the eighteenth century, such ground colours being generally thick and uneven. Hand painted ground colours, for instance the yellows of Meissen, or the so-called apple green of the Worcester Dr. Wall period, are usually variable and sometimes a little blotchy, showing that they were painted on by brush. It is truly miraculous how perfect some of these areas of painted ground colours can be. The later method of ground laid colours involved the application of powdered colour on to a prepared oiled surface, such ground laying at its best exhibiting a beautifully smooth even surface.

Many colours have changed their characters through the centuries, for instance eighteenth century copper green giving way to chrome green in the nineteenth century. Certain early colour effects are no longer possible with the banning of lead in the glazes and colours. Lead gave great depths of effect in certain colours but, of course, caused damage to the health of the potters.

As well as hand painting, many patterns could be transfer printed from the time of its first application to ceramics on Worcester porcelain in about 1755. The process of transfer printing is another one which many people have great difficulty in understanding but was done as follows:

An etched or engraved copper plate is heated and spread with one colour, say enamel black, the colour being rubbed into the copper. The surface colour on the copper is cleaned off with a spatula, further cleaned with a tow-filled cloth, leaving the colour remaining only in the incised lines of the copper. A toughened tissue paper is then covered with soapy water and put on to the still hot copper, to which it sticks; the paper covered copper is passed through the rollers of a press, rather like an old Victorian clothes mangle.

The paper is very carefully pulled off the copper; at this stage it is called a 'pull' and is in reverse impression to the pattern on the copper. The paper pull is pressed on to the piece to be decorated, which has meanwhile been warmed in an oven and covered with a sticky varnish so that the pull immediately sticks to the piece. There is no chance to slide it around to get it into a different position, so great skill is required in applying the pull. The paper is rubbed hard on to the piece, allowed to dry, washed off and the pattern, now back in the same position as it was on the copper, is transferred and ready to be fired in the kiln.

Such transfer printing can only be done in one colour, although the building up of different colours, as in Pratt printing, can be done in a rather laborious way, laying each small bit of separately printed colour piece by piece. It is possible to add colours by hand on to a print, tinting it or colouring it over, or filling in colours in outline prints.

Late in the nineteenth century lithographic printing came in. By this method it was possible to produce different colours in a single print much more cheaply than painting, transfer printing and tinting or washing in. To make it economical, however, a great quantity of the same subject had to be produced. This led to much of the poorest mass-produced rubbish of the late nineteenth to early twentieth century tourist trade, although at its finest, modern lithographic printing can be very good. Do not despise printing – good blue transfer printing being preferable to a poorly blue painted piece for instance.

I am often asked how it is possible to tell the difference between a painted and a printed piece. In the case of a lithograph it is relatively easy as when looked at with a powerful magnifying glass it is possible to see the dots that make up the pattern. With transfer printing it is not so easy, but look carefully at the individual lines which will be of level strength throughout their length. Painted lines will vary with the stroke of the brush, thin and thick or thick and thin. It is much harder to spot this when the pattern is in underglaze blue, as the glaze tends to make the blue blur. It might almost be best to suggest that you learn which subjects of a factory's production were

Plate **147**

A great range of coffee and teapots spanning nearly 300 years, giving some idea of the collecting scope offered. Details relate to the numbers in the key below the photograph.

1. Modern Spode.
2. Worcester, *circa* 1755.
3. Castleford, *circa* 1810.
4. Grainger, Worcester, *circa* 1835.
5. Wolfe, Liverpool.
6. Newhall, *circa* 1795.
7. Whieldon/Wedgwood, *circa* 1760.
8. Berlin, nineteenth century.
9. Chamberlain, Worcester, *circa* 1800.
10. Chinese, *circa* 1695.
11. Royal Worcester. *circa* 1875.
12. Worcester, *circa* 1758.
13. Bristol hard paste.
14. Spode, *circa* 1810.
15. Royal Worcester, *circa* 1870.
16. Chelsea, incised triangle period.
17. Worcester, *circa* 1785.
18. Staffordshire or Leeds.
19. Staffordshire agateware.
20. Staffordshire saltglaze.
21. Meissen, *circa* 1745.
22. Astbury type.
23. Wedgwood, nineteenth century.
24. Leeds creamware, *circa* 1770.
25. Staffordshire, dated 1790.
26. Jackfield type, *circa* 1745.
27. Staffordshire.
28. Staffordshire.
29. Chaffers, Liverpool.
30. Worcester, *circa* 1755.
31. Liverpool.
32. Staffordshire saltglaze.
33. Staffordshire saltglaze.
34. Turner, black basalt, *circa* 1800.
35. Staffordshire.
36. Worcester, *circa* 1770.

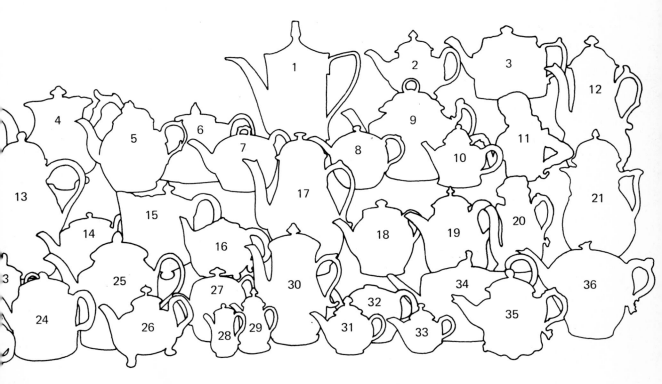

Plate **148**
Coffee pot made in Scotland for the Canadian market by John Marshall and Co. of Borrowstournness in Linlithgow, transfer printed with a popular Canadian sports subject. Height 9¼ in. Mark 'J. M. & Co.' and 'Canadian Sports' (occasionally the impressed mark 'Bo'ness' was used by this firm, which had a large trade with Canada, providing the brown wares and 'white granites' that the market required). *Circa* 1880.
Collection of Mrs. Elizabeth Collard, Montreal

printed and which painted, although this is somewhat begging the answer to the question.

I hope that these descriptions of making and decorating will encourage you to look with fresh eyes at your tea or coffee pot; to understand why the blue may be a bit runny, the shape a bit distorted, the glaze bubbled or pinholed. Remember always that it is really impossible to produce a piece of ceramics that is one hundred per cent perfect or exactly the same as every other piece, in the way of plastics. This is at the same time the drawback and the glory of ceramics, in the same way that no human body can be perfect nor like another one.

It is little wonder that the ancients thought that man was fashioned from the clay of the earth by the master potter.

Plate **149**
Royal Worcester 'Aesthetic' teapot, male on one side and female on the other, coloured in greens and yellows, and a skit on Oscar Wilde's Aesthetic Movement. The head removes to form the cover and the tea pours through a hole in the right hand. Height 6 in., *circa* 1880.
Dyson Perrins Museum

Plate **150**
Royle's self pouring teapot, a Doulton Victorian curiosity that satisfied the delight of the period in ingenious inventions.
Doultons

Plate **151** *(below)*
Two Martinware teapots and stands made in saltglaze stoneware by the Martin family of Southall, London potters. They made many stonewares in the style of ancient looking wares in the late nineteenth and early twentieth centuries. Notice the surface of the saltglaze resembling orange peel. Heights 6½ and 7 in.
Southall Public Library, photograph Leonard Taylor

Plate 152

An English 'Barge' teapot, the elaborate cover having a small teapot as the knob, covered with lustrous browny-black glaze, often incorrectly called 'Rockingham', with moulded and sprigged decoration. It is decorated with yellowy-white slip with the homely 'Home Sweet Home' clearly on the front. Such pots were favourite family gifts in the 1880's and are known as Barge pots because they were frequently found on canal narrow boats. Height 12 in., *circa* 1880.
Stoke-on-Trent City Museum

116

Plate **153** (*left*)
Very rare Mocha ware coffee pot, named after the typical 'Mocha tree' decoration, which can be very attractive. Such wares were made mainly in Stoke-on-Trent but imitations were made at Creil in France, and this pot might well be from the latter factory. Height 12⅝ in. Early nineteenth century.
Stoke-on-Trent City Museum

Plate **154** (*right*)
'Tourist' pot by Goss. Such pieces were made for the growing number of working class people able to go by railway to the seaside where they would purchase them for presents or as souvenirs. This one is of good quality although most were not. Height 6½ in. Printed mark: 'W H Goss' and a figure of a falcon. Late nineteenth century.
Stoke-on-Trent City Museum

Plate **155**
A beautiful tea kettle, covered with a thick Temmoku glaze; made by Shozi Hamada, one of the greatest of modern potters, while he was working with Bernard Leach at St. Ives. The pot has close affinities with Chinese wares of the Sung dynasty, which were a great influence upon Hamada and Leach. Height 11 in., length 10 in. *Circa* 1925.
Stoke-on-Trent City Museum

Plate **156**
Tea ceremony kettle by Tesshi
Nagano, made of cast iron with
reliefs of pine trees.
Japan Information Centre

Plate **157**
Modern Royal Copenhagen coffee
pot copying eighteenth century
style of shape and pattern,
painted in underglaze blue. It
might be thought a retrograde
step to reproduce old styles but
this is such a charming and well
made pot that no apologies are
made for illustrating it. Height
8¾ in.
Royal Copenhagen

Plate **158**
Four modern Wedgwood teapots,
all of which show echoes of old
ideas; no prizes for finding
derivative elements in the earlier
photographs in this book.

120

Plate **159**
Teapots made by the Homer
Loughlin China Company of
Newell, West Virginia, USA for
the present day American market.
Each pot has individuality.
Homer Loughlin China Co.

Plate **160** *(left)*
A 1972 teapot–the first prizewinner in the Tea Council's competition to find the perfect British teapot. Made by Anthony Plant of the North Staffordshire Polytechnic, it might be said to be traditional in shape with delightfully easy flow and fine proportions.

Plate **161** *(left)*
The second prizewinner in the Tea Council's 1972 competition, designed by Sybille Gerold, a student at the Royal College of Art. An exciting shape, inviting one to pick it up and pour from it.

Plate **162**
The third prizewinner in the Tea Council's 1972 competition, designed by Michelle Bernard of the Camberwell School of Art; this, the most originally modernistic of the three winners, may point the way to the future, or will we continue to have traditional type pots?

Bibliography

The Transactions of the English Ceramic Circle

Teapots and Tea by Frank Tilley,
Ceramic Book Company, 1957

The Tea Story by J. M. Scott, Heinemann, 1964

London Coffee Houses by Bryant Lillywhite,
George Allen and Unwin, 1963

English Pottery by Rackham and Read, 1924

Nineteenth Century Pottery and Porcelain in Canada
by Elizabeth Collard, McGill University Press,
Montreal, 1967

Index